Seymour & Parham

To Dr Jim Schneider
May God continue to bless you and
keep you.
Dr James D. Croom Sr.

Seymour & Parham

The Move of God Amid Relationship and Conflict

James D. Croone Sr.

Printed by
CreateSpace,
an Amazon.com company.

© 2016 by James D. Croone Sr.
All rights reserved. No part of this publication may be reproduced or transmitted in any form or by any means, whether electronic or mechanical, including photocopy, recording, or any information storage and retrieval system, without permission in writing from the copyright owner.

All scriptures are from
the Holy Bible, English Standard Version® (ESV®)
© 2001 Crossway,
a publishing ministry of Good News Publishers.
All rights reserved.

ISBN-13: 9781502499769
ISBN-10: 1502499762

Printed in the United States of America

Abstract

The aim of this thesis is to examine the relationship between William J. Seymour and Charles F. Parham by examining the societal norms of the nineteenth century and their impact on interactions across racial lines. This thesis will also give distinct attention to the Holy Spirit of God, who served as the framework and dialogue for both parties. This thesis will also assess the relationship between these two men through an impartial lens to determine how God's sovereign will withstood the divergence of cultural and human choices.

It is with great gratitude that I dedicate this book to my wife, Bobbie Croone, whose love and inspiration kept me writing, and my parents, for their unending love and support.

Table of Contents

Introduction · xi
    The Purpose of This Research · xiv
    The Plan of This Research · xv
    Chapter Analysis · xvi

Chapter 1   The Story · 1
    1.1 William Seymour · 2
    1.2 Charles Parham · 4
    1.3 Mr. Seymour, Meet Mr. Parham · · · · · · · · · · · · · · · · · 5
    1.4 Were Seymour and Parham Friends? · · · · · · · · · · · · · 9
    1.5 Separation Anxiety · 10
    1.6 Alma White · 13
    1.7 Julia Hutchins · 15
    1.8 The Building at 312 Azusa Street · · · · · · · · · · · · · · · 17
    1.9 Parham's Visit · 20
    1.10 Clara Lum and Florence Crawford · · · · · · · · · · · · · · 26
    1.11 William H. Durham · 27
    1.12 The End of Azusa · 29
Chapter 2   Understanding the Times · 31
Chapter 3   Relationship and Conflict · 38
    3.1 Carothers · 41
Chapter 4   "Raceology" · 46

Chapter 5   Seymour and Parham Reunited · · · · · · · · · · · · · · · ·55
Chapter 6   Conclusion ·60
            6.1 The Racial Component ·61
            6.2 The Cultural Component ·65
            6.3 The Theological Component · · · · · · · · · · · · · · · · · ·70

            Bibliography ·75
            About the Author ·83

Introduction

The Pentecostal movement, as well as other church denominations in the late nineteenth century, was subjected to or pressured into accommodating the racial segregation laws, also known as the Jim Crow[1] laws, that were in place at the time. Religious institutions appeared to be under more scrutiny than other organizations due to their emphasis on loving others and communing with one another, which could result in a great deal of fraternization among the races. Although scripture is replete with passages supporting unity and equality, many churches found ways to distort God's Word to make it meet the criteria of human law. Stetson Kennedy, the author of the book *Jim Crow Guide: The Way It Was*, offers the following examples of how admittance to the church and teaching the truth were prevented: "A Negro college professor in 1948 sought to join the white congregation of Atlanta's Unitarian Church, a relatively liberal denomination. His bid was refused, and the pastor was fired for seeking to admit him." Kennedy continues, "When Rev. Joseph Rabun, an ex-Marine chaplain, came back from World War II to espouse 'right supremacy, not white supremacy' from the pulpit of First Baptist church

---

1 "The purpose of Jim Crow was to keep African Americans subjugated at a level as close as possible to their former slave status. Together with its rigidly enforced canon of racial 'etiquette,' these rules governed nearly every aspect of life and outlined the draconian punishments for infractions as well." Jerrold M. Packard, *American Nightmare: The History of Jim Crow* (New York: St. Martin's Press, 2002), 1.

of McRae, Georgia, he was fired by the board of Deacons, which is dominated by the family of Senator Herman Talmadge."[2] These incidents were contributed to an environment of hate and prejudice. "The Pentecostal movement came into existence at the height of the Jim Crow era and it would have been an act of stunning moral courage for Pentecostals, especially those in the South, to have taken a consistent stand against the racism of the culture."[3]

The ideology of William J. Seymour and Charles F. Parham played a vital role in the Pentecostal movement, which has grown to comprise over three hundred million adherents worldwide. Although the theology of former times[4] may have perpetuated a message of separation, "the nonracist, integrated vision of Pentecostal faith that flourished for a brief time during the early years of the Azusa Mission had provided the movement with a working model of what nonracist Pentecostalism might look like."[5]

Skeptics and naysayers have disputed God's hand being a part of the movement.[6] The relationship between these two men was observed not only by the nonbelievers but by the religious community as well. Caricatures and cartoon parodies depicted both Seymour and Parham and called attention to their doctrines and their relationship. On February 21, 1907, a *Burning Bush* cartoon illustrated the split between the Pentecostal leaders. In this cartoon, Parham's head is affixed to the top of a jack-in-the-box, with the words "Gift of Tongues Los Angeles" written across the front of the box and the words "Our God Appointed Leader

---

2 Stetson Kennedy, *Jim Crow Guide: The Way It Was* (Boca Raton, FL: Florida Atlantic University Press, 1990), 197.

3 Douglas Jacobsen, *Thinking in the Spirit: Theologies of the Early Pentecostal Movement* (Bloomington: Indiana University Press, 2003), 262.

4 "As the movement became more institutionalized, patterns of Pentecostal organization unfortunately tended to become more segregated. This segregation of the movement followed the lines of race that defined the nation as a whole and specially emphasized the divide between white Americans and African Americans." Douglas Jacobsen, *Thinking in the Spirit: Theologies of the Early Pentecostal Movement* (Bloomington: Indiana University Press, 2003), 261.

5 Ibid., 262.

6 The term "movement" in this body of research refers to the Pentecostal movement.

Sept. 1906" written on the lower part of the box. A gentleman stands off to the side, motioning to release the lock. The next panel shows the lock being released and a startled man watching Parham's head flying off the box and Seymour's head popping out on a spring. W. C. Brand insists this: "The reports sent out by the tongue movement[7] are exaggerated and misleading. The movement has four serious faults: (1) A deceitful spirit (2) A self-sufficiency and unteachable spirit; (3) It causes strife and divisions among God's people: (4) It wrests the Scriptures and exalts feelings and experiences above plain Scripture."[8]

The boldness of Pentecostals made other denominations uneasy, which resulted in the hurling of insults. "In the 1910s and 1920s, many non-Pentecostal Christians called Pentecostal worship 'hell hatched free lovism.' They ridiculed Pentecostals because Pentecostals tended to be poor and uneducated."[9] It was not uncommon for those on the outside to accuse the Pentecostal community of being crazy: "Because of their free enthusiasm, Pentecostals were sometimes suspected of mental illness. In fact, one Azusa leader was arrested and tried before a lunacy commission. However, the judge dismissed the charge, saying that if the man were committed, half the Azusa community should also go to the asylum."[10]

Nevertheless, according to Olsen, "Pentecostals were successful evangelists partly because of their ability to minister to common people."[11] He also notes, "One woman, an Azusa convert, began a ministry to prostitutes

---

7 The term "the tongues movement" is typically interchangeable with the term "the Pentecostal movement," especially when those who oppose the Pentecostal movement use it.

8 W. C. Brand, "The Effects of the Tongues Movement," in *The Religious World Looks at Azusa Street 1906–1907: Skeptics & Scoffers*, ed. Larry E. Martin (Pensacola, FL: Christian Life Books, 2004), 57.

9 Timothy Paul Jones, *Christian History Made Easy* (Torrance, CA: Rose Publishing, 2009), 184.

10 Ted Olsen, "American Pentecost: The Story behind the Azusa Street Revival, the Most Phenomenal Event of the Twentieth-Century Christianity," *Christian History* XVII, no. 58 (1998): 11.

11 Ibid., 17.

and skid row alcoholics in Los Angeles."[12] Her weapon of choice was her guitar, which she would play while singing hymns to those who were downtrodden, in hopes of leading them to Christ. The many storms surrounding Seymour and Parham's relationship were in opposition to the prevailing societal norms.[13] In conjunction with the apparent blurring of racial boundaries, the dissolution of communal boundaries was becoming a vital part of the movement.

Despite the derision of those who disagreed with the doctrine of the Pentecostal movement, the achievements of Seymour and Parham are undeniable. It became evident that endless disputes over doctrinal differences and proprietorship did not manage to stop the move of God[14] nor sway the multitude of the move's followers.

THE PURPOSE OF THIS RESEARCH

The purpose of this research is not to malign or discount the doctrines of Seymour and Parham. Rather, it is an attempt to address the developing stages of the tension and doubts pertaining to the issues and the conflict surrounding their relationship—which in turn led to the events at Azusa Street. Although there is much detail available on various topics concerning Seymour and Parham, the relational aspect of their joint history will be the primary concern of this study, which aims to introduce a more compelling look into their lives and the societal norms surrounding these two men—who were on a mission to spread the gospel. By analyzing the

---

12 Ibid.

13 The word *norm* means "A group belief or rules that govern behavior in groups and societies."

14 The move of God here mirrors the epic moment that occurred in Acts 2. In this movement, the recipients of the Holy Spirit "were empowered for witness and began immediately magnifying the greatness of God." Clinton E. Arnold, *Acts* (Grand Rapids: Zondervan, 2002), 15. However, the move of God has also been defined as a supernatural posture of God. Many within the Pentecostal movement have expressed God's move as His Holy Spirit, which excites or stirs into action those who allow themselves to be filled with His presence. The Holy Spirit manifests in many ways—such as in a person speaking in unknown tongues.

principal figures, one can attempt to assess whether there was a move of God despite the impediments of humankind.

THE PLAN OF THIS RESEARCH

The historical method of this research will comprise of gathering relevant information pertaining to the topic. A brief hypothesis may be formed to better clarify the relationship between these two historical figures. The evidence collected is pertinent for this particular study, and I took great care to verify the authenticity of the sources used in this study. A historical approach will be employed in chapter 1 in order to create a more impartial view of the events leading to the end of the Azusa Street Mission. Brief sections of this historical approach will appear in the following chapters, but in those instances, it is merely used to set the background. The framework of this thesis, however, will rest primarily on the religious history, the social and cultural history, and the political history surrounding the lives of William J. Seymour and Charles F. Parham.

Many have sifted through information and hearsay to make sense of the involvement of these two men in the movement that has taken the religious community by storm. However, questions such as these still remain: Was Parham a racist? Did the Jim Crow laws play a significant part in the relationship between Seymour and Parham? If so, how did Parham's racism and the prominence of the Jim Crow laws affect the move of God? Did these affect the move of God at all? Though it may be proven that there was conflict in the relationship between Seymour and Parham, a movement was formed, and this movement prevailed.

Due to the era in which many of the events took place, race is an overarching theme in this story. The information compiled will provide helpful insight into not only the nature of the relationship between Seymour and Parham but also into the acts of humans and the will of God. We will also find that many who were a part of the movement agreed with the premise of the writers Guy P. Duffield and N. M. Van Cleave: "What God did through Luther in recovering the message of salvation, and did through

Wesley in recovering the message of holy life and service, He did through the early Pentecostal revivals in recovering the dynamism of the power and gifts of the Holy Spirit to the Church."[15]

CHAPTER ANALYSIS

Chapter 1 summarizes the full story of Seymour and Parham's relationship. Brief attention will be given to various segments of their lives as well as to their interactions with others who may have contributed to their relationship. Dates and background information—such as upbringing, education, and family—are pertinent in certain situations and provide context and significance to certain aspects of their joint narrative. The historical approach in this research relies on a range of authors who gave their insights into the accounts leading up to Azusa Street. The methodologies of the writers differ by their interests in or relationships to the individuals in the Pentecostal movement. They each have either a condemning or commending view of the movement. The various writers' accounts of the actual relationship between Seymour and Parham are—for the most part—consistent with one another.

Chapter 2 takes a concise look at the environment in which the story of Seymour and Parham took place. By examining the environment, one can better understand the reasoning behind the questionable human behavior of racism. Authors such as Albert J. Raboteau and Peter Randolph[16] aid this study of the environment by contributing insight into slave religion and plantation churches and by offering a broader look into the African American religious experience. The religious experience in 1906 bore an uncanny resemblance to behaviors exhibited during slavery. After a final analysis, it is apparent that the destructive laws and legislations of Jim

---

15 Guy P. Duffield and N. M. Van Cleave, *Foundations of Pentecostal Theology* (San Dimas, California: L.I.F.E. Bible College at Los Angeles, 1987), ix.
16 Albert J. Raboteau is professor of Religion at Princeton University and author of *Slave Religion: The Invisible Institution in the Antebellum South*. Peter Randolph is a former slave and author of *Sketches of Slave Life* (Michigan: Scholarly Publishing Office, University of Michigan Library, 2006).

Crow preserved the power of the former slave owners, even though slavery was illegal.

Chapter 3 gives a brief but detailed account of the meeting between Seymour and Parham and the ensuing circumstances surrounding the enrollment of Seymour into Parham's Bible college. This chapter also introduces Warren Faye Carothers, Parham's new comrade, who plays an intricate part in Seymour and Parham's relationship. Their willingness to tutor Seymour in his ministerial endeavors is compared to other historical events involving black and white relations in ministry.

The subject of chapter 4 is race and theology. The spiritual backgrounds of both Seymour and Parham are surveyed to better assess the ideology surrounding the movement. Further examination of Parham's belief system exposes his racial bias, which ratified segregation, leaving some in the Pentecostal movement to question the validity of his ministry. Following Seymour's progression through the holiness movement provides insight into his acceptance of Parham's "third blessing doctrine."

Chapter 5 concentrates on the reunion of Seymour and Parham. A more comprehensive inquiry into Parham's noticeable aversion for the happenings at the Azusa Street Mission is mounted. Parham's use of racial epithets is considered in relation to his association with Seymour and others in the movement. After a broader look into the meetings at Azusa, it becomes evident that the worship portion of the meetings drew the most criticism. They were portrayed as frolics, which caused many to view the movement as questionable. Faithful followers of the movement, however, reveled in what they believed to be a genuine move of God. Yet when biases coupled with faith are unveiled, the implications are shattering.

In light of the analysis, chapter 6 finalizes the observation of the relationship between Seymour and Parham through the following three lenses: the racial component, the cultural component, and the theological component. Each one of these factors allows one to see how segregation, biblical interpretation, and the misuse of God's Word can each play a substantial role in and outside of the religious community. This particular chapter defines racism and explains why it was the scourge of humanity and the church.

In addition to this thesis declaring or offering a concise resolution to the issue being addressed, how racism affected the relationship between Parham and Seymour and the Azusa Street Revival, this writer's hopes today's church would be "willing to put aside critical thinking and judgment until we know someone better. Taking the time to listen and understand the other person will help build bridges and dismantle barriers that often separate and isolate cultures."[17]

---

17 Kerby Anderson, *Christian Ethics in Plain Language* (Nashville: Thomas Nelson, 2005), 178.

One

The Story

Much of the information available on William Seymour speaks of him in ideal terms and describes him as humble, obedient, and controlled. For instance, H. V. Synan says, "Seymour's style of leadership was one of meekness. He encouraged freedom in the Spirit and often sat with his head covered behind the rough shoeboxes used as a makeshift pulpit. His speaking ministry was not in the tradition of black pulpit oratory but was more that of a teacher."[18]

Although there are many published reports and articles about the Azusa Street revival, very little has been mentioned about the initiator of the revival. There is little information about Seymour's background. It was not unusual for African Americans in that time to not receive acknowledgment in written form. Therefore, biographies and memoirs concerning African Americans were virtually unheard of in that period. Thus, historians today rely on secondhand accounts and speculations, which may at times harbor certain biases. On the other end of the spectrum, Charles Parham, a white man, was written about quite regularly. Some reports were unflattering, while others were commending. In regard to Parham's Apostolic Faith Movement, the widespread interest stemming

---

18 H. V. Synan, "William J. Seymour," in *The Dictionary of Pentecostal and Charismatic Movements*, ed. Stanley M. Burgess, Gary B. McGee, and Patrick H. Alexander (Grand Rapids: Zondervan Publishing House, 1988), 781.

from Parham's newspaper, *Apostolic Faith Movement*, earned him several thousand converts. Published writers at that time were primarily white.

Sarah Parham, Parham's wife, would later write a biography detailing her husband's exploits.[19] But it would have been highly unusual for Jenny Seymour, the wife of Seymour, to publish a similar work.

The story of Seymour and Parham is one of great importance, and it concerns a segment of church history that impacts many of us today. Therefore, an academic inquiry (as opposed to social activism) is needed to properly assess the narrative of these two individuals. To effectively examine Seymour and Parham's relationship today, one must view it through early-twentieth-century lenses. Therefore, in an effort to let the facts speak for themselves, this study will draw on information about twentieth-century conditions and on critical evaluations of the writings of various twentieth-century authors.

1.1 WILLIAM SEYMOUR

William Seymour was born on May 2, 1870, to Simon and Phillis Seymour, former slaves in Centerville, Louisiana. Very little is known about his childhood. At the age of ten, Seymour was enrolled in school. He had trouble reading and had not been taught to write due to the lack of proper education for people of color. Many of the blacks in the South in those days longed for an opportunity to head to the North, and Seymour was no exception. In 1895, at the age of twenty-five, Seymour moved to Indianapolis, Indiana, where he got a job as a waiter. He later was converted and attended the Methodist Episcopal Church, which was an African American congregation. He contracted smallpox and lost sight in his left eye. According to Larry E. Martin, "His face was so scarred by the disease that he wore a beard through the remainder of his life."[20]

---

19 Sarah E. Parham, *The Life of Charles F. Parham: Founder of the Apostolic Faith Movement* (New York: Garland Publication, 1985).
20 Larry E. Martin, *The Life and Ministry of William J. Seymour and a History of the Azusa Street Revival* (Pensacola, FL: Christian Life Books, 2006), 80.

Seymour perceived this illness as a divine call to enter into ministry. This resulted in his licensing and ordination as a minister with the Evening Light Saints Movement.[21]

Seymour is often described as a humble African American preacher, as the originator of the Pentecostal movement, and as the proprietor of the building located at 312 Azusa Street—which became known as the Azusa Street Mission. Craig Borlase provides the following brief but vivid portrait of Seymour and his impact on people: "Son of ex-slaves...blind in one eye...mentored, and then knocked down by a racist...verandas collapsing under the weight of people eager to get close to him as he prayed...thousands getting saved at the humble meeting hall in downtown Los Angeles."[22]

Secular publications also took notice of Seymour's revivals that took place at the Azusa Street Mission. On January 22, 2000, *Life* magazine printed a special edition of their magazine and included his revival in the list of the one hundred most momentous events in the previous century of American history. The Azusa Street revival ranked as the "sixty-eighth most important event to happen in America in the twentieth century."[23] Though the events at Azusa Street are a matter of record, the question of how these events came to be has not been fully answered. Rufus Sanders, a biographer, takes a balanced approach to the matter, giving some credit to each man. He describes Seymour as "an obscure black preacher who had moved to Los Angeles after having been initiated in the doctrines of Pentecostalism in Houston, Texas, by Charles Fox Parham, who had declared in 1901 that speaking in tongues was a sign of the Holy Spirit baptism."[24]

---

21 Synan, "William J. Seymour," 780.
22 Craig Borlase, *William Seymour: A Biography* (Lake Mary, FL: Charisma House, 2006,) x.
23 Rufus G. W. Sanders, *William Joseph Seymour: Father of the 20th Century Pentecostal/Charismatic Movement* (Sandusky, OH: Alexandria Publications, 2003), 1.
24 Ibid.

Many of the books written about the life of Seymour appear to be of one accord in regard to his character. Borlase maintains, "His life touches the six hundred million Pentecostals around the world today, not only because he preached well or promoted with skill but also because he simply followed Christ, taking those small steps of humility, obedience, and sacrifice."[25]

1.2 CHARLES PARHAM

James R. Goff Jr. depicts Charles Parham as an "American Pentecostal pioneer and author."[26] He says, "Parham formulated classical Pentecostal theology in Topeka, Kansas, in 1901 and thus deserves recognition as founder of the Pentecostal movement."[27] Sanders follows up a statement about Parham's remarkable contribution to the Pentecostal movement by averring, "I contend that without Parham there could have been no Seymour and, more important, no Azusa Street Revival."[28]

Born in Muscatine, Iowa, on June 4, 1873, Parham was one of William and Ann Marie Parham's five sons. "As an infant he suffered a virus probably encephalitis that weakened his childhood constitution and permanently stunted his growth."[29] He was later healed from his life-threatening illness when he was nine years old, and Parham's life was forever changed. His announcement that God had called him to preach did not fall on deaf ears. His passion for ministry prompted him to seek greater endeavors, which would eventually change the church of his time. In January 1901 Parham's notoriety began when students started speaking in tongues at his Bible school in Topeka, Kansas.[30]

---

25 Borlase, *William Seymour: A Biography*, xi.
26 J. R. Goff Jr., "Charles Fox Parham," in *Dictionary of Pentecostal and Charismatic Movements*, ed. Stanley M. Burgess, Gary B. McGee, and Patrick H. Alexander (Grand Rapids: Zondervan Publishing House, 1988), 660.
27 Ibid.
28 Sanders, *William Joseph Seymour*, 61.
29 Goff Jr., "Charles Fox Parham," 660.
30 Cecil M. Robeck Jr., *The Azusa Street Mission and Revival* (Nashville: Thomas Nelson, Inc., 2006), 40.

After Topeka, Parham's ministry developed a strong adherence to glossolalia.[31] Though Parham's ministerial skills lacked refinement, he possessed a strong devotion to discerning and following God's will for his life.[32]

1.3 MR. SEYMOUR, MEET MR. PARHAM

There are divergent opinions about whether Seymour or Parham was the true leader of the Pentecostal movement. Did the movement start with Parham at Stone's Mansion in Topeka Kansas, on New Year's Day in 1901? Or did it start with Seymour on Azusa Street in Los Angeles, California, in 1906? Synan and Fox state, "Clearly, Parham greatly affected Seymour's personal life and theology."[33] Many in the Pentecostal movement, however, insist that "William Seymour was an African American Minister, and initiator of the Pentecostal religious movement."[34] Not only was the Azusa Street revival a milestone in the Pentecostal movement, according to some, it was also a springboard for controversy, discord, and uncertainty. Much of what came about in the latter years allegedly arose from the relationship between Seymour and Parham. Seymour and Parham met in 1905 when a lady by the name of Lucy Farrow introduced Seymour to Parham. Farrow was an African American woman who was the niece of Frederick Douglass, a prominent abolitionist. She had apparently experienced the baptism of the Holy Spirit during one of Parham's meetings.

---

[31] This is the definition of speaking in tongues, and it is defined as follows: "A spiritual gift involving ability to speak in foreign language(s) not previously studied or to respond to experience of the Holy Spirit by uttering sounds which those without the gift of interpretation could not understand." Trent C. Butler. "Gift of Tongues," in *Holman Bible Dictionary*, ed. Trent C. Butler (Nashville: Holman Bible Publishers, 1991), 1356.

[32] Alan F. Bearman and Jennifer L. Mills, "Charles M. Sheldon and Charles Parham: Adapting Christianity to the Challenges of the American West," *Kansas History: A Journal of the Central Plains* 32 (2009): 117.

[33] Vinson Synan and Charles R. Fox Jr., *William J. Seymour: Pioneer of the Azusa Street Revival* (Alachua, Florida: Bridge-Logos Foundation 2012), 61.

[34] John Hunt, The Essential Writings of the American Black Church (Chattanooga, TN: AMG Publishers, 2008), 708.

She shared her testimony with Seymour, prompting him to attend the meetings with her to hear the teachings of Parham.[35] After the meetings, Seymour would search through his Bible to see if Parham was correct concerning the practice of baptism. "He finally concluded that Parham's position on baptism in the Holy Spirit with the Bible evidence of speaking in other tongues made sense as the best interpretation of the biblical facts."[36] However, his eagerness to experience the baptism of the Holy Spirit was obstructed "because Parham did not allow for a racially integrated altar."[37] This is evident in that "Parham not only seated black people separately in the rear of his meetings, but also prohibited interracial mingling at the altar afterward."[38] The altar was the place designated at the time to seek the baptism of the Holy Spirit, and Seymour was denied this experience because of his race. This could be due to the fact that the Jim Crow[39] laws were strict about the fraternization of whites and blacks, even in church settings.[40]

In addition to his unfailing attendance at Parham's church services, Seymour enrolled in Parham's Bible college.[41] According to Synan, the course consisted of a ten-week intensive Pentecostal indoctrination.[42]

---

35 "The meetings that Parham held in Houston were segregated meetings, in keeping with local cultural expectations and local legislation. Whites were given the primary seats in the auditorium or sanctuary, while African Americans were required to sit or stand in the rear." Robeck Jr., *The Azusa Street Mission and Revival*, 46–47.
36 Ibid., 46.
37 Ibid.
38 J. D. Nelson, "For Such a Time as This: The Study of Bishop William Seymour and the Azusa Street Revival" (PhD diss., University of Birmingham, England, 1981).
39 The Jim Crow laws are a set of laws initiated between 1877 and 1965 and are designed to make African Americans second-class citizens. These laws impacted nearly every aspect of the lives of African Americans, regulating where they could attend school, eat, live, gather, work, and in some cases, whom they could marry.
40 Kennedy, *Jim Crow Guide*, 197.
41 "With thirty-four students, Parham began Bethel Bible College, a Bible school that would emphasize the Holy Spirit baptism." James R. Goff Jr., Fields unto Harvest: Charles F. Parham and the Missionary Origins of Pentecostalism (Fayetteville, AR: University of Arkansas Press, 1988), 65.
42 Vinson Synan, *The Holiness-Pentecostal Movement in the United States* (Grand Rapids: Eerdmans Publishing, 1971), 103.

Parham's school was not the first Bible school Seymour attended. While working as a waiter in Cincinnati, Seymour attended Martin Wells Knapp's Bible school—name God's Bible School—where he was taught holiness theology. The axiom for God's Bible School was "back to the Bible."[43] Unlike Parham's school, Knapp's Bible school permitted blacks and whites to sit and study together. There are differing accounts about Seymour's enrollment and the seating arrangement at Parham's holiness school. One account says the following: "Eagerly, Seymour sought out Parham and begged to be admitted to the school."[44] Another account states that Farrow, a former governess of Parham in Topeka, Kansas, "interceded on Seymour's behalf, and Parham conceded that Seymour could have a space in the classroom. He would have to take his seat in the hall outside the classroom door."[45]

Parham's acceptance of Seymour's admittance to the school also elicits conflicting views among current authors. Unlike Robeck's account of what appears to be Parham calmly conceding to Seymour, Harvey Cox states, "Parham hesitated. A Ku Klux Klan sympathizer, he did not feel ready to welcome this obviously earnest, but just as obviously black, seeker."[46] Despite his personal bias, Parham enrolled Seymour in his school, possibly with the hope of instructing him in the faith so that he could spread the movement to the black districts. "He told Seymour he could listen to the lectures seated on a chair outside an open window. On rainy days, he was permitted to sit inside the building, but in the

---

43 It was during this time that Seymour contracted smallpox, which was running rampant in Cincinnati at the time. Seymour incurred some of the scarring that usually comes to survivors. As a result, he lost one eye and it was replaced with an artificial one." Robeck Jr., *The Azusa Street Mission and Revival*, 35. Seymour was convinced that God was chiding him for refusing a call to His ministry.
44 Harvey Cox, *Fire from Heaven: The Rise of Pentecostal Spirituality and the Reshaping of Religion in the Twenty-First Century* (Reading, MA: Addison-Wesley Publishing Company, 1995), 49.
45 Robeck Jr., *The Azusa Street Mission and Revival*, 47.
46 Cox, *Fire from Heaven*, 49. To the issue of Parham as a Ku Klux Klan Sympathizer; cf. Rufus G. W. Sanders, "*William Joseph Seymour,*" 109; Craig Borlase, *William Seymour: A Biography,*" 166.

hallway outside the classroom, with the door left ajar."[47] Borlase sheds a different light on the subject and states, "Seymour sat outside the classroom and listened to the master through the door that was left ajar," and says, "A defining image, perhaps? Certainly it's one with multiple interpretations and one that places front and center the key question of the hour: was Parham a racist?"[48] Larry Martin says, "In what sounds more like an excuse than an apology, Mrs. Parham explained, 'In Texas, you know, colored people are not allowed to mix with white people as they do in some other states.'"[49]

Segregated seating in the classroom would not have been considered unusual then or in previous times. Milton C. Sernett states the following: "James W. C. Pennington (1808-70), better known as the 'fugitive Blacksmith,' tried to attend class at Yale in 1845 but had to stand outside its lecture rooms."[50] Notwithstanding the many differences between authors concerning Parham's attitude toward the admittance of Seymour into his Bible school, one must take into account that the Jim Crow laws were a factor in the state of Texas. Not only were African Americans prohibited from sitting and studying in the classroom, "the Jim Crow racial codes in place in Houston at this time prohibited African Americans and Whites from worshipping together."[51] Goff states, "Parham, sensitive to the local Jim Crow statutes and yet sympathetic to the spread of the Pentecostal doctrine among blacks, admitted Seymour to the Bible school but provided separate seating."[52] This limited much of Seymour's participation in class. "Although the curriculum called for students to engage

---

47 Cox, *Fire from Heaven*, 49.
48 Borlase, *William Seymour*, 82.
49 Parham, *The Life of Charles F. Parham*, 137.
50 Pennington further remarks, "One wonders if he caught any presentations on moral theology, for he could have taught Yale's faculty something of the practice of day-to-day moral reasoning." James W. C. Pennington, "Great Moral Dilemma," in *African American Religious History: A Documentary Witness, Second Edition*, ed. Milton C. Sernett (London: Duke University Press, 1999), 81.
51 Sanders, *William Joseph Seymour*, 72.
52 James R. Goff Jr., *Fields White unto Harvest: Charles Parham and the Missionary Origins of Pentecostalism* (Fayetteville, AR: University of Arkansas Press, 1988), 107.

in hands-on, practical ministry, Seymour would not be able to minister to whites. He would have to find a way to do his work among blacks."[53]

However, "despite limitations imposed on him due to his race and his lack of formal education, Seymour's deep hunger for the things of God and keen intellect allowed him to excel in Bible school studies."[54] According to Harvey Cox, "Seymour was not discouraged. He listened through the window and prayed ardently for the new baptism of the Spirit and the gift of tongues."[55]

1.4 WERE SEYMOUR AND PARHAM FRIENDS?

Friendship is defined as "a distinctively personal relationship that is grounded in a concern on the part of each friend for the welfare of the other, for the other's sake, and that involves some degree of intimacy."[56] Friendship has been used to describe Seymour and Parham's relationship in many publications. The Jim Crow laws, however, made it virtually impossible for blacks and whites to appear as friends in public. Under no conditions did interracial etiquette permit a black male to shake hands with a white male. This would imply a form of equality. Nor was it tolerable for the two to sit and eat together.[57] "If they did eat together, Whites were to be served first, and some sort of partition was to be placed between them."[58]

Borlase states, "Parham stood alongside Seymour and others when they approached the black districts, but as soon as they were back on his home turf, segregation was back in play, and Parham disappeared off to the front."[59] Borlase, viewing this as hypocritical, does not hesitate to

---

53 Robeck Jr., *The Azusa Street Mission and Revival*, 47.
54 Martin, *The Life and Ministry of William J. Seymour*, 93.
55 Cox, *Fire from Heaven*, 50.
56 Bennett Helm, "Friendship," in *The Stanford Encyclopedia of Philosophy*, ed. Edward N. Zalta, (2009) http://plato.stanford.edu/archives/fall2009/entries/friendship.
57 Kennedy, *Jim Crow Guide*, 212.
58 Ibid.
59 Borlase, *William Seymour*, 84.

say this: "Parham was clearly prejudiced."[60] Whether or not one would view this as hypocritical or bigoted, it is evident that Parham was priming Seymour for ministry.

Robeck asserts that "during the time he [Seymour] was a student in Parham's school, Seymour remained silent on the issues with which he disagreed."[61] This is plausible, considering Seymour's social setting. Others, however, insist that Seymour and Parham "sometimes disagreed rather vociferously."[62] According to Kennedy, the author of *Jim Crow Guide*, this type of variance would run counter to the law, which states that blacks must "never assert or even intimate that a White person is lying. Never impute dishonorable intentions to a White person. Never lay claim to, or overly demonstrate, superior knowledge or intelligence."[63] The penalty for this type of defiance was extreme.[64] Seymour never voiced any opinions concerning Parham's theology, but whether this was due to his humble disposition or to his fear remains unclear.[65]

1.5 SEPARATION ANXIETY

All indications pointed to Parham grooming Seymour to carry the apostolic message to the African Americans in Houston.[66] According to Larry

---

60 Ibid.
61 Robeck Jr., *The Azusa Street Mission and Revival*, 49.
62 Sanders, *William Joseph Seymour*, 72.
63 Kennedy, *Jim Crow Guide*, 216-217; cf. Jerrold Packard. *American Nightmare: The History of Jim Crow*, (New York: St Martin's Press, 2002), 170.
64 "Blacks who violated Jim Crow norms risked their homes, their jobs, and even their lives. Whites could physically beat Blacks with impunity. Blacks had little legal recourse against these assaults because the Jim Crow criminal justice system was all-White: police, prosecutors, judges, juries, and prison officials. Violence was instrumental for Jim Crow. It was a method of social control. The most extreme forms of Jim Crow violence were lynchings." David Pilgrim, "What Was Jim Crow?" Jim Crow Museum of Racist Memorabilia (2011), www.ferris.edu/jimcrow/what.htm; cf. Kennedy, Jim Crow Guide, 170; Packard, American Nightmare, 85.
65 Frank Bartleman describes William Seymour as "A black man, blind in one eye, very plain, spiritual, and humble." Frank Bartleman, *Azusa Street* (New Kensington, PA: Whitaker House, 1982), 38.
66 "Carothers would later write that he and Charles Parham had been 'arranging to send [Seymour] out with the message among the African population of Texas.'"

E. Martin, "God willed something better for His humble servant, and He was soon to set those grand plans in motion."[67] Seymour had only been attending Parham's Bible college for a month before he received a request from Julia Hutchins to come to Los Angeles to pastor her mission at Ninth Street and Santa Fe Street. Neely Terry, a woman who visited a church that Seymour was pastoring in Houston, piqued her interest in Seymour. Terry was quite taken by Seymour's godly disposition and his spiritual prerequisites. "She told Seymour that in her home church in Los Angeles, a black congregation, a certain sister Hutchins had recently preached a revival and had sounded much like him."[68] When Terry went back to her home church in Los Angeles,[69] she described Seymour's humble disposition and godly character to her pastor, Julia Hutchins. "Pastor Julia Hutchins and the small congregation were so impressed and inspired with the testimony of Mrs. Terry that they quickly raised the train fare and sent for Seymour."[70] Seymour was excited about the invitation and was certain that God had ordered his steps in this undertaking. Martin states, "No doubt, Seymour was anxious to go west, not only to share the faith, but also to find the 'promised land' of racial equality he had not found in his northern sojourns and certainly did not find in Texas."[71] Sanders affirms, "Seymour, who was having a strained relationship with Reverend Parham, sought his blessing, but accepted the invitation as a mission from God himself. He resolved to leave Houston without delay."[72]

Regarding his invitation to Los Angeles, Seymour wrote the following: "It was a divine call that brought me from Houston to Los Angeles.

Robeck Jr., *The Azusa Street Mission and Revival*, 50.
67 Martin, *The Life and Ministry of William J. Seymour*, 94.
68 Cox, *Fire from Heaven*, 50.
69 "The church was connected with the Southern California Holiness Association, was founded by and pastored by Julia W. Hutchins." Synan, "William J. Seymour," 780.
70 Sanders, *William Joseph Seymour*, 73.
71 Martin, *The Life and Ministry of William J. Seymour*, 94.
72 Sanders, *William Joseph Seymour*, 73.

The Lord put it on the heart of one of the saints in Los Angeles to write to me that she felt the Lord wanted me to come there, and I felt that was the leading of the Lord. The Lord provided the means and I came to take charge of a mission on Santa Fe Street.[73]

Seymour later likened his call to that of Paul. According to Cox, "To Seymour, her [Hutchins's] call reminded him of the vision that had once appeared to St. Paul when a man called to him and said, 'Come to Macedonia and help us.'"[74] Robeck maintains this: "Seymour would later write that he came to Los Angeles at the request of 'the colored people,' because they wanted him 'to give them some Bible teaching.'"[75] Therefore, he accepted the invitation. "The next step for Seymour was to inform Parham of his invitation to Los Angeles. Parham had been telling his students that they should pray that the Lord would send openings for them to serve in ministry, and they were instructed to follow God's leading in this matter."[76] Robeck writes this: "When Seymour shared the invitation with Parham, Parham was very resistant. Carothers (Parham's field director for the *Apostolic Faith Movement*)[77] would later write that he and Charles Parham had been 'arranging to send [Seymour] out with the message among the African population of Texas.'"[78] Much of the literature pertaining to Seymour's departure from Houston describes the disappointment of Parham and Carothers.

---

[73] James S. Tinney and Stephen N. Short, eds., *In the Tradition of William J. Seymour: Essays Commemorating the Dedication of Seymour House at Howard University* (Washington, DC: Spirit Press, 1978), 6.

[74] Cox, *Fire from Heaven*, 50.

[75] Robeck Jr., *The Azusa Street Mission and Revival*, 62.

[76] Ibid., 50.

[77] "Carothers, a future executive presbyter of the Assemblies of God was, by his own admission, an ardent segregationist." Robeck Jr., *The Azusa Street Mission and Revival*, 48. "[Carothers] justified racial segregation in the south by arguing that although all humanity shared one blood (Acts 17:24–26), God had created a multiplicity of nations that God subsequently divided along color lines. He believed that the United States had been intended by God to become a nation for whites, just as Africa was intended to be a continent set apart by God for those with black skin." Cox, *Fire from Heaven*, 46.

[78] Robeck Jr., *The Azusa Street Mission and Revival*, 50.

"Carothers admitted that when Seymour suddenly 'announced that he was called of God to go to California,' that the Texas workers were 'disappointed somewhat.'"[79]

Parham and Carothers had not intended to preach the apostolic faith message so far so soon, but "they were further opposed to his going until he had been baptized in the Holy Spirit."[80] Despite their opposition to Seymour leaving, it would appear that Parham and Carothers knew that it was inevitable. Putting aside disagreements, Carothers initiated a ceremony, which necessitated laying hands on Seymour. "Parham also issued ministerial credentials to Seymour, and raised an offering to help offset the Azusa leader's travel expenses to Los Angeles."[81] Cox maintains that Seymour borrowed "the train fare from Parham and set off for his own Macedonia, eager to preach the good news of the gift of tongues and the imminent coming of the glorious New Jerusalem."[82] However, although Parham's disappointment was not enough to cause Seymour to deny what he believed to be a call from God, Borlase insists that Seymour "left Houston with Parham's prediction of failure weighing him down."[83]

1.6 ALMA WHITE

Seymour made full use of his trip to Los Angeles by making stops at well-known holiness missions along the way; one in particular was the Pillar of Fire Church (a Wesleyan holiness denomination)[84] in Denver, Colorado, led by Mrs. Alma White.[85] According to sources, White was an acrimonious antagonist of the Pentecostal movement and the tongues movement. The fact that her husband left her to join the Pentecostal movement

---

79 Martin, *The Life and Ministry of William J. Seymour*, 94.
80 Robeck Jr., *The Azusa Street Mission and Revival*, 50.
81 Synan and Fox Jr., *William J. Seymour: Pioneer of the Azusa Street Revival*, 61.
82 Cox, *Fire from Heaven*, 50.
83 Borlase, *William Seymour*, 99.
84 The name varies; in different publications, it is alternately called the Pillar of Fire sect, Pillar of Fire Headquarters, and the Pillar of Fire Training School.
85 Alma White is said to be the first female bishop of the church.

might have initiated her distaste for the movement and Seymour.[86] Martin cites that her depiction of "Seymour's appearance and demeanor, set a pattern of biased stereotypes against the preacher that continue even till this day."[87] She made critical remarks about his clothes being shabby and his odor being repugnant. She went so far as to say that he was possessed by demons, and she claimed that when he prayed, she felt the presence of snakes around her.[88] Alma White's unflattering remarks about Seymour's attire provided Morton Kelsey, the author of *Tongue Speaking: An Experiment in Spiritual Experience*, with the fervor to say, "He was one-eyed, unprepossessing in manner, and rather careless about his person."[89] "It was a well-established fact Mrs. White's descriptions were shaded by her prejudicial opinion of colored people and the Pentecostal movement."[90] In Susie Cunningham Stanley's book *Feminist Pillar of Fire: The Life of Alma White*,[91] White made an attempt to start a mission in California to convert the Christians based in the Los Angeles area.[92] The mission itself was unsuccessful; however, she did place many pastors in the churches she began in the surrounding area.[93] Despite the

---

86 Alma White, *My Heart and My Husband* (Zarephath, NJ: Pillar of Fire Publishers, 1923).

87 Martin, *The Life and Ministry of William J. Seymour*, 95.

88 For more information, see Alma White, *Demons and Tongues* (Zarephath, NJ: Pillar of Fire Publishers, 1936).

89 Morton Kelsey, *Tongue Speaking: An Experiment in Spiritual Experience* (Garden City, NY: Doubleday, 1964), 63.

90 Sanders, *William Joseph Seymour*, 75.

91 Susie Cunningham Stanley, *Feminist Pillar of Fire: The Life of Alma White* (Cleveland: The Pilgrim Press, 1993); see also Bishop Alma White, *The Ku Klux Klan In Prophecy* (Zarephath, NJ: Pillar of Fire Church, 1925).

92 "She reserved a particular distaste for Christians based in the Los Angeles." Borlase, *William Seymour*, 90.

93 One church in particular on Eighth Street and Maple Street served another purpose. Ironically, "Within a year of Seymour's visit to White's holiness center in Colorado, her own Pillar of Fire congregation on 8th and Maple atrophied and died, unable to pay the rent." He adds, "In a pleasant twist of fate, the building remained in use as a place of religious worship, soaking up the overflow from those unable to cram into another local congregation, the one on Azusa Street." Borlase, *William Seymour*, 90.

mockery he received from White, Seymour boarded the train heading to Los Angeles, anticipating God's next move.

1.7 JULIA HUTCHINS

On February 22, 1906, William Seymour reached Los Angeles, California. His first sermon was preached at the mission on Ninth and Santa Fe Street in April of 1906.[94]

Seymour began services in the holiness church on February 24. The chosen text for his sermon came from Acts 2:4, which says, "And they were all filled with the Holy Spirit and began to speak in other tongues as the Spirit gave them utterance." While Seymour had not yet experienced speaking in tongues, he adamantly taught that speaking in tongues was the evidence of the baptism of the Holy Spirit Although Hutchins held some of the same doctrinal viewpoints as Seymour, the issue of speaking in tongues was not one of them. It "was too new, and too disturbing and controversial, for these simple holiness people who had not yet accepted tongues as a doctrine of the church."[95] Seymour's doctrinal view concerning speaking in tongues clearly ran counter to a group that "believed that they were sanctified, they already had the Holy Spirit baptism."[96] There has been some speculation that Hutchins locked Seymour out of the church immediately after his controversial sermon, prohibiting him from any further involvement with the church. This supposition, however, is refuted by Robeck, who says, "That is probably not the case. Seymour began preaching there on Saturday evening, February 24. He probably conducted the regularly scheduled services on Sunday, February 25; Tuesday, February 27; and Friday, March 2."[97] According to Charles Shumway,[98] Seymour

---

94 Mrs. Julia Hutchinson pastored the mission on Ninth Street and Santa Fe Street.
95 Sanders, *William Joseph Seymour*, 84.
96 Martin, *The Life and Ministry of William J. Seymour*, 140.
97 Robeck Jr., *The Azusa Street Mission and Revival*, 62.
98 "In 1914 Charles Shumway, a Methodist minister who was writing a baccalaureate for the University of Southern California, interviewed William J. Seymour." Robeck Jr., *The Azusa Street Mission and Revival*, 27.

preached several meetings at Hutchins's mission before he and his accumulated followers were locked out. Although some writers insist that the Holiness Association acted on its own presupposition, others insist that Hutchinson, who notified the president of the association, may have heavily swayed their decision.

According to Martin, "President J. M. Roberts, the director of the Southern California Holiness Association, and several holiness ministers were brought into the church, perhaps partially at least due to the insistence of W. H. McGowan, who, with his family, had been attending the meetings. Seymour was given a chance to defend himself and his doctrine."[99] Martin continues, "According to one witness, Roberts was glad Seymour was seeking the baptism and he hoped the visitor from Texas would soon receive."[100] According to Robeck, Roberts said this to Seymour: "When you receive it, please let me know, because I am interested in receiving it too."[101] Yet Roberts's holiness colleagues were fully committed to the belief that the baptism of the Holy Spirit and sanctification were one and the same, and they rejected any belief that another experience existed. Nevertheless, "because of opposition from the Holiness Association, Hutchins locked the door, and Seymour was forced to find refuge in the home of Richard Asberry on Bonnie Brae Avenue."[102] The Asberrys[103] were sympathetic to Seymour's new doctrine.

Seymour had now found himself far from home with a tough message to sell: "The doctrine of tongues."[104] It had become evident that "most holiness people, including Mrs. Hutchins, equated baptism in the Spirit with sanctification, and they did not see the ability to speak in tongues as

---

99 Martin, *The Life and Ministry of William J. Seymour*, 140.
100 Ibid.
101 Robeck Jr., *The Azusa Street Mission and Revival*, 64.
102 Synan, "William J. Seymour," 780.
103 The spelling of the name Asberry differs in various publications and is sometimes spelled Asbury or Asbery.
104 The doctrine that considers speaking in tongues as the evidence of the Pentecostal experience.

connected to it at all."[105] The invitation by the Asberrys later proved to be a blessing for Seymour. The Asberry home had a history of conducting evangelical services. "On Monday nights, the group would hold a gospel concert in front of the house, attracting curious families from the neighborhood. As the crowd grew, they would be invited inside for an evangelistic service."[106] Now the Asberry home would add a new segment to its history, and Seymour would be noted as the initiator of a passionate revival. "After several weeks of prayer meetings in the Asberry home, Seymour and others received the sought-for tongues experience, an event that sparked an intense revival."[107] The news of this extraordinary event flourished into an inordinate number of meetings at the Asberry home. "The strange events at Bonnie Brae Street drew so much attention that Seymour was forced to preach on the front porch to crowds gathered in the streets."[108] Curious bystanders and seekers could be seen peering into the windows of the Asberry home, hoping to catch a glimpse of people speaking in tongues or receiving the baptism of the Holy Spirit. Sanders notes, "When people would get near the house, many would fall under the anointing power of God. For three days many were healed and saved."[109] "It was at this point that Seymour began his search for a bigger building, anticipating a mighty outpouring of the Holy Spirit."[110]

1.8 THE BUILDING AT 312 AZUSA STREET

Many are in agreement that Seymour's character was not tarnished by the unusual turn of events that he encountered after leaving Houston.

---

105 Robeck Jr., *The Azusa Street Mission and Revival*, 62–63. Julia Hutchinson eventually accepted Seymour's theology of speaking in tongues. In the October 1906 issue of *The Apostolic Faith* newspaper, Hutchinson gives an account of God speaking to her in her backyard, telling her to leave Los Angeles in September and go to Africa. Borlase, *William Seymour*, 107.
106 Martin, *The Life and Ministry of William J. Seymour*, 129.
107 Synan, "William J. Seymour," 780.
108 Synan and Fox Jr., *William J. Seymour*, 34.
109 Sanders, *William Joseph Seymour*, 87.
110 Synan and Fox Jr., *William J. Seymour*, 34–35.

Cox insists this: "Because of his controversial teaching, Seymour—from Louisiana by way of Houston—had been locked out of one church by an irate pastor and denied access to others. But he and his tiny company continued to meet in kitchens and parlors, praying that God would renew and purify a Christianity they believed was crippled by empty rituals, dried-up creeds, and the sin of racial bigotry."[111] Seymour's countenance throughout this ordeal, according to Borlase, remained humble. "If this troubled Seymour, he had clearly nurtured an innate talent for maintaining a premium quality poker face, as there are no accounts to contradict the image of him doing anything other than prayerfully, peacefully waiting to see what God might do next."[112] Seymour and his band of followers sought out a place to worship. Their search led them to an old building located in downtown Los Angeles—the building was located at 312 Azusa Street.[113] The property had served as an African Methodist Episcopal Church at one time and was later used as a stable and warehouse, as evidenced by the dirt floor that "seemed to flow almost out onto the unpaved street."[114]

According to A. C. Valdez, it was "a boxy, two-story, wooden building which, except for a tall Gothic window on the front of the second floor, looked like the general store in many a small, western town."[115] The area surrounding the building was not attractive: "stables, wholesale houses, lumber yards and a tombstone shop surrounded the old church building."[116] The saloons in the area perpetuated unpleasant activities. The condition of the building made cleanup difficult but necessary, and cleanup included, among other issues, the task of removing hay and other debris from the

---

111 Cox, *Fire from Heaven*, 46.
112 Borlase, *William Seymour*, 105.
113 The property deed description said this: "Lots seven and eight of Orange Tract, City of Los Angeles, County of Los Angeles, State of California." (Mortgage Deed, 31 December 1930, Book 10511, pp. 227–278, Los Angeles County, California)
114 Borlase, *William Seymour*, 123.
115 A. C. Valdez Sr. with James F. Scheer, *Fire on Azusa Street* (Costa Mesa, CA: Gift Publications, 1980), 19.
116 Martin, *The Life and Ministry of William J. Seymour*, 158.

previous proprietor. However, "for $8 a month it ceased its incarnation as a storage facility for construction materials and became the new home of the still unnamed congregation."[117] Seymour took up residence on the second floor, and the first floor was designated as the place of worship. Not all were satisfied with the accommodations, because the dirt floor flowed out into the street and the rain made it impossible for one to walk on the floor without slipping or sloshing around in the mud. Cara Lum, a devoted follower, noted that "it was the most humble place I was ever in for a meeting."[118] April 14, 1906, the day before Easter, was the day that the first service was held. According to Borlase, "The first meeting at 312 Azusa Street drew a hundred people. The second drew more, and the third even more."[119] Despite the inadequacy of the surroundings, Seymour "presided over this gentle pandemonium with tact and an impressive capacity for personal diplomacy."[120] Seymour was not a run-of-the-mill Pentecostal preacher. He resembled a teacher—he was meek and plain. He would often be found kneeling and praying in front of a makeshift pulpit formed with two wooden shoe crates, one on top of the other, veiled with a cotton cloth. According to Cox, "Within days, the word was out all over Los Angeles. Something was happening in the little church in the colored section of town."[121] Although the predominant lure was people speaking in tongues, Seymour did not make speaking in tongues the primary significance of the Azusa Street Mission. He would often admonish his hearers and say, "Don't go out here talking about tongues: talk about Jesus."[122]

The experiences being felt by the congregants of the Azusa Street Mission consisted of shouting, shaking, speaking in tongues, and falling

---

117 Nelson, "For Such a Time as This," 192.
118 Clara Lum, "Clara Lum Writes Wonders," *The Missionary World* (1906), 2.
119 Borlase, *William Seymour*, 125.
120 Cox, *Fire from Heaven*, 57.
121 Ibid., 57.
122 Vinson Synan, "William Seymour," *Christian History* 19, no. 1 (2000): 17–19, ebscohost.com.firma.northwestu.edu/ehost/delivery.

down "like an army slain on the battle field."[123] These unstructured reactions began to catch the attention of reporters. "On April 18, 1906,[124] the *Los Angeles Times* ran a front page story on the revival, 'Weird Babel of Tongues, New Sect of fanatics is breaking loose, wild scene last night on Azusa Street, gurgle of wordless talk by a sister.'"[125] In addition to the remarkable events taking place at the mission, the races were also unified. According to Cox, "In retrospect the interracial character of the growing congregation on Azusa Street was indeed a kind of miracle. It was, after all, 1906, a time of growing, not diminishing, racial separation everywhere else. But many visitors reported that in the Azusa street revival, blacks and whites and Asians and Mexicans sang and prayed together."[126]

Frank Bartleman wrote this: "The color line was washed away in the blood of Christ."[127] Dan Thrapp of the *Los Angeles* Times corroborates this phenomenal occurrence: "The meetings were attended by people of every group on the face of the earth."[128] In a span of two months, attendance had grown to nearly thirteen hundred people, and those who were unable to fit inside sought solace out on the sidewalk. According to reports by the *Los Angeles Daily Times*, the sixty-foot by forty-foot room "was crowded almost to suffocation."[129]

1.9 PARHAM'S VISIT

Nearly every periodical and book written concerning Parham's visit to the Azusa Street Mission in Los Angeles reports that his trip began and

---

123 Martin, *The Life and Ministry of William J. Seymour*, 179.
124 April 18, 1906, was the day of the San Francisco earthquake. "Two earthquakes shook Los Angeles within ten minutes of each other." Larry E. Martin, *The Life and Ministry of William J. Seymour and a History of the Azusa Street Revival* (Pensacola, FL: Christian Life Books, 2006), 167.
125 Hunt, ed., *The Essential Writings of the American Black Church*, 708.
126 Cox, *Fire from Heaven*, 58.
127 Frank Bartleman, *Azusa Street* (New Kingston, PA: Whitaker House, 1982), 51.
128 Dan L. Thrapp, "Pentecostal Sects to Convene Here," *Los Angeles Times*, Sept. 9, 1956.
129 "Women with Men Embrace," *Los Angeles Daily Times*, Sept. 3, 1906.

ended on a bitter note. James R. Goff Jr. states, "Seymour had written faithfully during the summer with glowing reports of the revival's progress and clearly anticipated that his own work would reach unparalleled heights when the leader of the Apostolic Faith arrived in Los Angeles for a mass city-wide campaign."[130] However, time did not permit Parham to come at that time, so he sent an additional five workers to visit the Azusa Mission. On August 27, Seymour wrote a letter to Parham informing him of the arrival of Anna Hall (presumably a worker sent by Parham) and insisting that he come to be a part of a great union revival. In this letter, Seymour wrote the following: "Sister Hall has arrived, and is planning out a great revival in this city, that shall take place when you come. The Revival is still going on here that has been going on since we came to this city. But we are expecting a general one to start again when you come, that these little revivals will all come together and make one great union revival."[131] Seymour's acknowledgement of Parham as his spiritual father and the "Projector"[132] of the movement prompted him to invite Parham to preach a union revival at Azusa.

In the fall of 1906, Parham finally arrived in Los Angeles. According to Sanders, "Parham said that to his utter surprise and astonishment, he found conditions even worse than he had anticipated."[133] Parham did not hold back his distaste for what he called "darky camp meeting stunts" and "fits and spasms of spiritualists."[134] Moreover, he denounced the "mixing of the races prevalent in the services."[135] He later published his

---

130 Goff Jr., *Fields White unto Harvest*, 113.
131 "Seymour to Parham, 27 August 1906. This source is problematic since it only appears in Mrs. Parham's account and the original cannot be found in PSD." Footnote from Goff Jr., *Fields White unto Harvest*, 214.
132 According to Craig Borlase, "Parham's ego, it seems, was in rude health, and it was about this time that he chose for himself a new title. Instead of leader, pastor, or founder, Parham decided that he was to be known as Projector of the Apostolic Faith Movement." Borlase, *William Seymour* (Lake Mary, FL: Charisma House, 2006), 81.
133 Sanders, *William Joseph Seymour*, 108.
134 Synan, "William Seymour," 3.
135 Larry E. Martin, *The Topeka Outpouring of 1901: Eye Witness Accounts of the Revival that Birthed the Twentieth-Century Pentecostal Movement* (Joplin, MO: Christian Life Books, 1997), 18.

findings at the Azusa Street Mission. He wrote this: "Men and women, whites and blacks knelt together or fell across one another; frequently a white women, perhaps of wealth and culture, could be seen thrown back into the arms of a 'buck nigger,' and held tightly thus as she shivered and shook in freak imitation of Pentecost. Horrible, awful shame! [Azusa Street was too much like a] darky revival."[136]

According to Borlase, on this particular October evening when Parham entered Azusa Street, he witnessed people "shaking, jerking on an invisible line beyond their control. As the power of the Spirit increased through laying on of hands, many fell to the floor, unable to stand under the weight of so intense an experience."[137] Joyner insists race was the more determining factor in Parham's discourse: "Even more than the faking of experiences, Parham was appalled by the unusual social and racial integration. Parham admired the Ku Klux Klan,[138] and especially objected to racial mixing or mingling during worship and at the altar."[139] Clearly the issue of "race mixing" was not a doctrine that Seymour and Parham shared. According to Sanders, "Seymour believed that the Azusa renewal was true Christianity, a renewal where all barriers of race, color, gender, class and nationality were, in his view, divinely abolished."[140] Parham's view of "racial mixing" was starkly different from Seymour's view. Parham held the belief that the flood in Genesis 1 was due to the mixing of races and that the choosing of Noah was based on his being pure. Parham viewed racial mixing as the great sin of humanity.[141]

---

136 Cox, *Fire from Heaven*, 61.
137 Borlase, *William Seymour*, 163.
138 "Like Alma White, Parham had ties to the Ku Klux Klan." Iain Mac Roberts, *The Black Roots and White Racism of Early Pentecostalism in the USA* (London: MacMillan Press, 1988). See also Goff Jr., *Fields White unto Harvest*, 157.
139 Rick Joyner, *Azusa Street: The Fire That Could Not Die*. 1996, www.openheaven.com/library/history/azusa.htm. Martin, *The Life and Ministry of William J. Seymour*, 269.
140 Sanders, *William Joseph Seymour*, 109.
141 Charles F. Parham, *The Everlasting Gospel* (Baxter, Springs, KS: Apostolic Faith Bible College), 111–117. See also Goff Jr., *Fields White unto Harvest*, 103.

Nevertheless, the man under whom Seymour had studied, the man whom Seymour described to others as "God's leader,"[142] was rejecting what Seymour deemed to be a move of God. In fact, Parham solidified his denouncement by positioning himself in the center of a meeting and "deliver[ing] a verdict that few can misunderstand."[143] He said, "God is sick to His stomach!"[144] Aside from Parham's racial epithets, his condemnation of the altar workers' deceitful practices appeared to be warranted. Their overzealous desire for people to receive the baptism of the Holy Spirit drove them to lay hands on people, "jerking their chins, massaging their throats, and telling them to repeat certain sounds over and over or faster and faster until they spoke in tongues."[145]

Seymour acknowledged Parham's charges of hypocrisy and deception. Joyner asserts, "Seymour realized that some were faking the manifestations, and believed that these were tares sent by the devil to foul the field of wheat. Even so, he held to the biblical wisdom to let the wheat and tares grow up together. He knew that if he tried to root out the tares, the wheat would also be uprooted—if he stopped that which was not real, he would also quench the Spirit and the work that was real."[146] Concerning the intense experiences being exhibited, Seymour later wrote this: "The Lord knocked Paul down and he got up trembling and saying 'Lord, what wilt thou have me to do?' The Lord knocked all worldly wisdom out of Paul. That is the reason He knocked so many people down here, to take the worldly wisdom out of them. Paul was a man full of the wisdom and knowledge of this world, but when he got the baptism with the Holy Ghost, he was able to tell us about true wisdom and true knowledge."[147]

---

142 "When Parham accepted the invitation from Seymour to conduct a city-wide revival, he was announced in the Azusa paper as 'God's Leader of the Apostolic Faith Movement.'" "Letter from Brother Parham," *The Apostolic Faith*, Sept. 1, 1906.
143 Borlase, *William Seymour*, 165.
144 Charles William Shumway, "A Study of 'The Gift of Tongues'" (master's thesis, 1914).
145 Robeck Jr., *The Azusa Street Mission and Revival*, 140.
146 Rick Joyner, *Azusa Street: The Fire That Could Not Die*.
147 Borlase, *William Seymour*, 163.

Parham's dissatisfaction with the activities at Azusa Street and the perceived ineptness of the leadership prompted him to attempt to convince Seymour "to resign and turn the reins over to him. However, the Azusa congregation rejected Parham's racism and his claim to leadership, and Parham was asked to leave."[148] Seymour's response to Parham's rants is not found in any writings. One could speculate, however, that the Jim Crow laws that were in place may have had some bearing on Seymour's lack of response. One must also take into account Seymour's character, which has been described as not lacking in meekness. Martin notes the only recorded response from Seymour: "Seymour lamented, 'you know, it is my color.'"[149] This turn of events caused an irrevocable break between the two, but Parham would not leave Los Angeles without a fight. He acquired a space at the Woman's Christian Temperance Union building, and he conducted his own mission with the intent of stopping and thwarting the work that Seymour felt God had called him to do. Parham managed to draw some of the members away from the Azusa Street Mission, and when Parham decided to leave Los Angeles, he assigned W. F. Carothers as his successor at the mission. Carothers's racial views were even more extreme than Parham's views. Despite the attempts of Parham and Carothers, Seymour and the Azusa Street revival continued to grow with vigor.

"Soon visitors from around the nation and from foreign lands journeyed to Los Angeles to receive their own Pentecostal experience."[150] Parham's anger continued to burn for some time. Borlase says, "Parham's anger of the first night continued, for weeks, months, even years."[151] In the midst of Parham's campaign to discontinue the revival at Azusa Street, Parham was arrested and charged with sodomy in 1907 in San Antonio, Texas. "A story in the *San Antonio Light* on that day broke the first genuine

---

148 Sanders, *William Joseph Seymour*, 109.
149 Martin, *The Life and Ministry of William J. Seymour*, 270.
150 Synan, "William J. Seymour," 781.
151 Borlase, *William Seymour*, 167.

scandal in Pentecostal history."[152] One source said this: "The details of the case are extremely sketchy and filled with innuendo and rumor."[153] There are differing thoughts on the aftermath of Parham's public humiliation. Martin insists the following: "Although he denied the accusations until his death, his ministry never fully recovered. Carothers and Howard Goss disfellowshipped Parham from the organization he had founded."[154] In fact, "for decades, Pentecostal historians did not even mention his name."[155] On the other hand, Bearman and Mills claim that despite "the charges of racism and unsubstantiated accusations of sexual misconduct, he maintained a loyal following throughout his ministry and he continues to be seen as the father of the modern Pentecostal movement."[156] According to Goff, Parham's case mysteriously vanished from the San Antonio newspaper, and no formal indictment was ever filed.[157] Goff goes on to say this: "The lack of clear acquittal in San Antonio along with rumors of Parham's impropriety over the past six months[158] combined to create the public impression of guilt."[159] Though less reliable, the religious newspapers did more to hurt Parham's ministry than the San Antonio papers. "The religious press was more detailed. The most explicit of the accounts offered a mountain of 'evidence' aimed at discrediting the Kansas evangelist and putting him out of business."[160]

---

152 Goff Jr., *Fields White unto Harvest*, 136; cf. *Apostolic Faith* 1 (1906): 136.
153 Goff Jr., "Charles Fox Parham," 661.
154 Martin, *The Life and Ministry of William J. Seymour*, 271-272.
155 For example, see Stanley H. Frodsham, *With Signs Following* (Springfield, MO: Gospel Publishing House, 1946). "Frodsham actually edited the Parham name out of quotations." Footnote from Martin, *The Life and Ministry of William J. Seymour*, 272.
156 Bearman and Mills, "Charles M. Sheldon and Charles F. Parham," 116.
157 Goff Jr., *Fields White unto Harvest*, 137.
158 This statement is referencing Parham's outspoken displeasure with the mixing of races at Azusa Street, his resignation out of frustration because of his loss of authority, and the failing relationship between himself and Carothers.
159 Goff Jr., *Fields White unto Harvest*, 138.
160 Ibid. See also *Supplement to the Zion Herald*, July 26, 1907 and *Burning Bush* 6, Sept. 19, 1907.

1.10 CLARA LUM AND FLORENCE CRAWFORD

Although Seymour was euphoric about the Holy Spirit and its manifestation being experienced at the Azusa Street Mission, "he could not foresee two major issues that would soon change the whole entire situation—Seymour's decision to marry Jennie Evans Moore, and the controversial preaching of William H Durham."[161] Seymour would soon come to realize that Parham was not the only one turning on him. Clara Lum, an influential sister in his ministry, deserted him in 1908, taking the mailing list for the *Apostolic Faith* paper. This damaged Seymour's leadership with the movement because Lum was the editor of *Apostolic Faith*. Lum headed straight to the Portland Apostolic Faith Mission to assist Florence Crawford.[162] "Because he was neither able to produce the paper without Lum's expertise, nor promulgate it without the national and international lists, Seymour's message could no longer be conveyed to his constituents."[163] To add insult to injury, "in June 1908, the fourteenth edition of the paper was printed without the familiar 'Apostolic Faith' mast on the front page."[164] The July and August 1908 edition had the following statement: "We have moved the paper, which the Lord lain on us to begin at Los Angeles, to Portland, Oregon, which will now be its headquarters."[165] Borlase states this: "While Seymour had never used the paper to solicit donations, the paper had been a vehicle through which they had come."[166] Lum, however, took a more forward approach: "Some have asked how to send money offerings. Stamps are very acceptable. If necessary to get a money order, it can be made payable to the APOSTOLIC FAITH, PORTLAND ORE."[167]

---

161 Ithiel C. Clemmons, *Bishop C. H. Mason and the Roots of the Church of God and Christ* (Bakersfield, CA: Pneuma Life Publishing, 1996), Kindle edition.
162 Reverend Florence Crawford was the founder of *The Apostolic Faith*, Portland, Oregon.
163 Synan and Fox Jr., *William J. Seymour*, 135.
164 Martin, *The Life and Ministry of William J. Seymour*, 279.
165 *The Apostolic Faith*, July and August 1908.
166 Borlase, *William Seymour*, 197.
167 *The Apostolic Faith*, July and August 1908.

Many have speculated that Seymour's marriage to Jennie Evans Moore—an African American woman—prompted Lum's betrayal.[168] Clemmons noted that Seymour had sought counsel from his friend and mentor Charles H. Mason. "According to Mason, Seymour told him that Clara Lum (a White woman) had privately made it clear that she had fell in love with Seymour and wanted him to propose marriage to her. Seymour had tentatively considered the possibility and discussed the matter in its early stages with Mason, who advised him to not even think about the idea."[169] Due to the demise of all the parties involved, it is virtually impossible to substantiate this assertion. However, considering the time and the vigorous opposition to racial integration, an interracial marriage would have been disastrous socially and might have endangered the lives of both parties.

"Seymour tried to print at least one edition, and perhaps more, of the paper, but it was impossible to continue without the mailing lists or the financial contributions that had been misdirected to Portland."[170] Seymour attempted to rectify the damage by traveling to Portland—only to be met with resistance from Crawford and others. "While attendance at the Azusa Street Mission remained healthy throughout most of 1908, by the beginning of 1909 it had entered a steady decline."[171] In the end it could be said, as avowed by Borlase, "With two swift hands and a train ticket, Clara Lum castrated the Azusa Mission. End of story."[172]

1.11 WILLIAM H. DURHAM

The year 1911 brought more misery for Seymour, but this time it was from a former and ardent supporter William H. Durham. "While Seymour was away from Los Angeles, touring the East, Durham was invited to

---

168 Robeck Jr., *The Azusa Street Mission and Revival*, 310.
169 Clemmons, *Bishop C. H. Mason and the Roots of the Church of God and Christ*, Kindle edition. Locations 1028-1030.
170 Martin, *The Life and Ministry of William J. Seymour*, 280.
171 Robeck Jr., *The Azusa Street Mission and Revival*, 311.
172 Borlase, *William Seymour*, 196; cf. Robeck Jr., *The Azusa Street Mission and Revival*, 310.

preach at the Azusa Mission."[173] Being a former follower of Seymour, Durham was well aware of the doctrine being taught at the mission; nonetheless, "Durham's message seems to have had a certain appeal to the minority of Seymour's followers who had been raised in white Baptist and Presbyterian churches with more Calvinistic theologies."[174] Unbeknownst to Seymour, Durham did not hold to the belief that sanctification was the second definite work of grace. Rather, he held "that God sanctified the believer at conversion by placing them 'in Christ,' then the believer matured in holiness as they grew in grace."[175] According to Cox, "Durham had undercut the entire theological rationale for the revival."[176] In fact, Durham's intentions became evident when he "asked for a show of hands from those who supported the continuation of the 'revival' under his leadership. The response was overwhelmingly in favor of Durham."[177] Seymour decided to padlock the doors of the mission to prevent Durham and his followers from entering the building. Durham was given a temporary place by Frank Bartleman[178] to conduct his services, and "on Sundays, one thousand would attend his meetings."[179] The Azusa Street Mission had dwindled considerably. Parham was enraged by Durham's sanctification doctrine—so much so that "Parham prayed in January 1912 that God would prove the proper doctrine by taking the life of whichever prophet taught in error. When Durham died suddenly six months later, Parham felt assured that God had properly answered his prayer."[180]

---

173 Synan and Fox Jr., *William J. Seymour*, 131.
174 Cox, *Fire from Heaven*, 62.
175 Robeck Jr., *The Azusa Street Mission and Revival*, 316.
176 Cox, *Fire from Heaven*, 62.
177 Robeck Jr., *The Azusa Street Mission and Revival*, 317.
178 "Frank Bartleman worked largely with the Holiness churches in Los Angeles, but he was always looking for the latest work of God. He also attended the mission at Azusa Street and established another at Eighth and Maple Streets." Frank Bartleman, *Azusa Street* (New Kensington, PA: Whitaker House, 1982), 170.
179 Martin, *The Life and Ministry of William J. Seymour*, 289.
180 Goff Jr., *Fields White unto Harvest*, 152.

1.12 THE END OF AZUSA

The strain on Seymour became too much for him to bear. Men and women he had trusted now sought to discredit and humiliate him. Although Seymour championed the belief that the evidence of the baptism of the Holy Spirit was speaking in tongues, he found it perplexing that his white colleagues could speak in tongues and still loathe their fellow black Christians. This led Seymour to adopt a new theory: speaking in tongues was not as sure a sign of the baptism of the Holy Spirit as the eradication of racial prejudice. Cox says, "The early white Pentecostals disagreed. Uncomfortable under black leadership and embarrassed by the opprobrium heaped on them for 'worshipping with niggers,' they finally opted to reject the interracial fellowship and keep tongues."[181] It had become evident, according to Synan, that "the struggles with Parham, Crawford, and Durham effectively ended Seymour's major role of leadership in the Pentecostal movement."[182] Also at an end was his "dream of an interracial Pentecostal movement that would serve as a positive witness to a racially segregated America."[183] The betrayals and backbiting Seymour received from his white colleagues seems to have encouraged him to segregate the mission. He went so far as to amend the doctrines, discipline, and constitution of the church: "The Apostolic Faith Mission shall be carried on in the interest of and for the benefit of the colored people of the state of California, but the people of all countries, climes, and nations shall be welcome."[184]

Racial tensions increased, and the congregation began to wither, until just a few faithful members remained. Many were coaxed away from the mission by Durham,[185] including most of Seymour's staff. Seymour's staff at the time was primarily white, which may have contributed to the

---

181 Cox, *Fire from Heaven*, 63.
182 Synan, "William J. Seymour," 781.
183 Ibid.
184 Nelson, For Such a Time as This, 264.
185 Borlase, *William Seymour*, 227. A reported 70 percent of Seymour's staff defected from Azusa.

additional revision that insisted that the leadership of the church be made up of colored people. Borlase maintains, "Seymour never gave up on unity and merely acted in this way to protect his own flock from those who threatened to abuse privilege for their own purposes."[186]

In the summer of 1922, John Matthews, a known opponent of the tongues movement, was in Los Angeles attending a conference. Someone alerted him to Seymour's presence in Los Angeles. Matthews claimed that Seymour looked tattered and fatigued. "On September 28, 1922, William suffered a heart attack. Later that same day, around three o'clock, he suffered a second one. He was dead at fifty-two years of age."[187] According to Martin, "His last message was 'a plea for love among brethren everywhere.'"[188] However, his last words were spoken "without a struggle. Smiling radiantly...'I love my Jesus so.'" [189] Seymour's wife attempted to lead the failing ministry but to no avail. After her death in 1936, the mission was lost in 1938 due to massive debts. Eventually, "the Mission on Azusa Street was torn down after the Assemblies of God, a direct descendant of the Azusa movement, showed no interest in acquiring it."[190]

Many scholars and authors have painted Seymour as an extraordinary example of a man who loved God and people. His advocacy for the unity of the brethren of Christ can be evidenced in his Doctrines and Discipline of the Azusa Street Apostolic Faith Mission: "Our colored brethren must love our white brethren and respect them in truth so that the word of God can have its free course, and our white brethren must love their colored brethren and respect them in truth so that the Holy Spirit won't be grieved. I hope we won't have any more trouble and division of spirit."[191]

---

186 Borlase, *William Seymour*, 228–229.
187 Sanders, *William Joseph Seymour*, 123.
188 Martin, *The Life and Ministry of William J. Seymour*, 330.
189 Ibid.
190 Sanders, *William Joseph Seymour*, 130.
191 William J. Seymour, *Doctrines and Discipline of the Azusa Street Apostolic Faith Mission*.

Two

Understanding the Times

Seymour and Parham's relationship was set against the backdrop of a social system based on segregation and the Jim Crow laws. From 1876 through 1965, states and localities within the United States ordained legislation known as the "Jim Crow laws," and "its central purpose was to maintain a second-class social and economic status for blacks while upholding a first-class social and economic status for whites."[192] Any relationship beyond labor or servitude between blacks and whites was prohibited. According to the *Dictionary of American English on Historical Principles*, the name *Jim Crow* had rather unusual roots. "Jim Crow was the name of a minstrel routine (actually Jump Crow) performed beginning in 1828 by its author, Thomas Dartmouth ('Daddy') Rice, and by many imitators, including actor Joseph Jefferson. The term came to be a derogatory epithet for blacks and a designation for their segregated life."[193] The Jim Crow laws were ubiquitous—segregating restaurants, drinking fountains, restrooms, public schools, facilities, and transportation. The US military was also not exempt from segregation. In fact, states rarely honored their agreement to pay black soldiers their full pensions. Simon Seymour, William Seymour's father and a veteran of the Civil War, became gravely ill. He

---

192 Packard, *American Nightmare*, vi.
193 Sir William Alexander Craigie and James R. Hulbert, eds., *A Dictionary of American English on Historical Principles* (Chicago: University of Chicago Press, 1944).

made his request for permanent disability in 1890. "In June of 1891, Simon was described as 'weak, feeble, and hardly conscious' by the New Orleans doctor who refused to sign off on a full pension for Simon, in spite of a mixed bag of symptoms including rheumatism, diarrhea, and an affliction of the eyes."[194] Eventually, the physician "recommended a limited pension because of piles, but said Seymour's general appearance was 'healthy.'"[195] Simon Seymour died shortly after—on November 14, 1891.

The Jim Crow era led to an unorthodox form of etiquette and social behavior between the races. This etiquette was primarily constructed for blacks and other minorities. The closeness—or lack thereof—in Seymour and Parham's relationship is not clearly shown in the few books written about the two. The interracial etiquette that governed the interactions between whites and blacks during the Jim Crow era made it virtually impossible for a genuine relationship to form between members of the two races. Prior to the Jim Crow laws, free people of color were subject to the Black Codes,[196] which were designed to limit the freedom of blacks. The Louisiana Black Code states this: "Free persons of color ought never to insult or strike white people, nor pressure to conceive themselves equal to the white; but on the contrary they ought to yield to them in every occasion, and never speak or answer to them but with respect, under penalty of imprisonment according to the nature of the offense."[197]

A curfew was also in place for blacks; they were not allowed to be out at night, unless accompanied by a white person. "Southerners, whites and Negros alike, having been steeped for generations in the atmosphere engendered by interracial etiquette, usually know precisely-almost instinctively-just what is expected of them in all situations."[198] According to

---

194 Borlase, *William Seymour*, 35. See also Joanna Jenkins, *General Affidavit*, June 14, 1893, Simon Seymour Pension File, National Archives and Records Admiration.
195 Martin, *The Life and Ministry of William J. Seymour*, 56; see also Surgeon's Certificate, (Seymour Pension File, National Archives and Records Admiration).
196 The Black Codes were enacted soon after the Civil War—in 1865 and 1866—mainly in the South.
197 Kennedy, *Jim Crow Guide*, 205.
198 Packard, *American Nightmare*, 203.

Packard, "Jim Crow, the laws that set into stone an already existing way of life, infiltrated Southern life almost faster than could be comprehended."[199] Therefore, laws enforcing interracial etiquette may not have been much of a shock to Seymour or Parham, who were both from the South. Their Southern roots make it likely that they had already accepted these rules as normal behavior. But there were areas outside of the South where people were not accustomed to this social outlook. However, Seymour and Parham resided well within the areas impacted by the Jim Crow laws. From 1866 to 1948, twenty-seven Jim Crow laws were passed in Houston, Texas. Racism was the crux of the Jim Crow laws. It was not unusual for one to open a morning paper and see the word *nigger* or *darkies* used to describe African American people. This may explain why in published reports Parham used phrases such as "buck nigger" and "darkie revival" to describe his dislike of the interracial mixing at Azusa Street. At the time, these phrases would not have been much of a shock to white readers. Black communities and districts were commonly known as "Dark town," "Nigger town," or "Black Bottom."[200] Blacks and whites were never to be seen as equals; if a white person were to befriend a black person, it would typically be viewed as a paternalistic act. Supporters of the Jim Crow laws, especially the Ku Klux Klan, were resolute in maintaining that America was the white man's country and that the "forefathers never intended that it should fall into the hands of an inferior race."[201]

The fear of treating blacks as equals may have inspired interracial unions and sexual relations. Of course, interracial sexual contact between black men and white women was illegal and socially unacceptable. According to the Jim Crow laws, it was interpreted as rape. The consequences were severe and violent for the African American party—typically death by lynching. Kennedy states, "If you are a nonwhite man, your very life may depend upon your ability to keep a safe distance from white women in segregated territory. Generally speaking, it can be dangerous to get within

---

199 Ibid., 85.
200 Ibid., 103.
201 Kennedy, *Jim Crow Guide*, 26.

arm's reach of one. In fact, the further you stay away from them, the safer you will be."[202]

William J. Seymour's marriage to Jennie Moore, an African American woman, is said to have sparked jealousy in Clara Lum, a white woman, who had admitted her love to Seymour and who wanted him to marry her. If Seymour and Lum had married, Seymour's story and life would have come to an abrupt end. The Jim Crow system was enforced by terror, intimidation, and violence. When blacks were perceived by whites to be achieving any form of economic or political advancement, a mob would step in and terrorize the blacks. For instance, residential segregation was enforced by bombing the homes of blacks who had moved outside of their communities. White real estate brokers who sold or rented properties to blacks were also the targets of these bombings.[203] It was not uncommon for racist groups, especially the Ku Klux Klan,[204] to murder or persecute whites who stood up for blacks or befriended them. According to Kennedy, the Christian church was also guilty of this type of intimidation: "Glen Taylor (then Senator of Idaho) discovered [this] when he sought in 1948 to enter a Negro church at Birmingham, Alabama, through a door marked 'Negro Entrance,' instead of the one marked 'White Entrance' which had been set up by the police for the occasion of his appearance there. He was charged with disorderly conduct, fined, and sentenced to 39 days in jail. Upon appeal, federal courts upheld his conviction, and the US Supreme Court refused to review it."[205]

The tentacles of the Jim Crow laws literally squeezed the very essence out of the gospel, rendering it ineffective. According to some—such as white ministers—Christian doctrine had long before embraced segregation, and in fact, God was seen as an ardent supporter of racism. Whites

---

202 Ibid., 210.
203 Packard, *American Nightmare*, 107.
204 "The Ku Klux Klan was spawned from defeated Southerners' need to keep former slaves under white control, its rationale largely fear of a black uprising in the chaotic aftermath of emancipation." Packard, *American Nightmare: The History of Jim Crow*, 125.
205 Kennedy, *Jim Crow Guide*, 197.

were considered the chosen people, and blacks were cursed. Charles Parham's racial ideology—particularly his Anglo-Saxon theory—was actually perpetuated through ministers who where slaveholders. Long before the Jim Crow laws were in place, plantation churches were oppressing blacks. "The Gospel was so mixed with slavery, that the people could see no beauty in it, and feel no reverence for it."[206] Slaveholders would twist biblical passages to suit their need to control their slaves. "The prominent preaching to the slaves was, 'Servants, obey your masters. Do not *steal* or *lie*, for this is very wrong. Such conduct is sinning against the Holy Ghost, *and is base ingratitude to your kind masters, who feed, clothe and protect you*'" (emphasis mine).[207] A former slave by the name of Charlie Van Dyke reported that sermons preached by the slaveholders never mentioned Jesus.[208] "Slavery was not only accepted as an economic fact of life, but defended as a positive good, sanctioned by Scripture and capable of producing a Christian social order based on the observance of mutual duty, slave to master and master to slave."[209] The segregated seating arrangements in the plantation churches resembled those of many white churches during the time of Seymour and Parham's encounter. Reverend Peter Randolph[210] describes in his autobiography a church called "Brandon's Church." He says, "And there the white Baptists worshiped. Edloe's[211] slaves sometimes went there. The colored people had a

---

206 Peter Randolph, "Plantation Churches: Visible and Invisible," in *African American Religious History: a Documentary Witness, Second Edition*, ed. Milton C. Sernett (London: Duke University Press, 1999), 64.
207 Ibid.
208 Raboteau, *Slave Religion: The Invisible Institution in the Antebellum South*, 214.
209 Ibid., 152.
210 Reverend Peter Randolph (1825–1897) was birthed as a slave on the Brandon Plantation, which was owned by Carter Edloe, and was in Prince George County, Virginia. Randolph—after the death of his master in 1844 and after he and sixty-six other slaves received their emancipation, which was ordered by their master in his will—fulfilled what he believed was a call from God to preach Christianity to his fellow slaves. Randolph later became a licensed minister for the Baptist Church.
211 Edloe was the name of Peter Randolph's master; Randolph was one of the eighty-two slaves owned by Edloe.

very small place allotted to them to sit in, so they used to get near the window as they could to hear the preacher talk to his congregation."[212] Slave preachers would risk their own lives to tend to the spiritual well-being of their fellow slaves. "The slaves yearned for greater spiritual refreshing in their communal meetings and often stole away to Jesus by assembling in the quarters, swamps, and 'hush harbor.' There they could hold meetings with preachers of their own."[213] These types of religious gatherings were forbidden without the approval of their masters. If caught, the slaves were whipped, but the slaves considered this as suffering for Christ's sake. Randolph asserts, "In some places, if the slaves are caught praying to God, they are whipped more than if they had committed a great crime. The slave-holders will allow the slaves to dance, but do not warrant them to pray to God. Sometimes, when a slave, on being whipped, calls upon God, he is forbidden to do so, under threat of having his throat cut, or brains blown out."[214]

The gatherings served as a temporary safe haven and an escape from the harsh reality of the pain and suffering imposed on them by their masters. Anderson Edwards, a former slave, cites a song, which expresses suffering and hope. He said, "We prayed a lot to be free and the Lord done heered us. We didn't have no songbooks and the Lord done give us our songs and when we sing them at night it jus' whispering so nobody hear us. One went like this:

'My knee bones am aching,
My Body's rackin' with pain,
I 'lieve I'm a chile of God,
And this ain't my home,
'Cause Heaven's my aim.'"[215]

---

212 Randolph, "Plantation Churches," 64.
213 Ibid., 63.
214 Ibid., 68.
215 Raboteau, *Slave Religion*, 218.

At these hidden religious meetings, the slave preacher "usually commence[d] by calling himself unworthy, and talk[ed] very slowly, until feeling the spirit, he gr[ew] excited, and in a short time, there f[ell] to the ground twenty or thirty men and women under its influence."[216] The passionate worship exhibited at the Azusa Street Mission mirrors that of the religious gatherings held by the slave preachers. With the exception of the racial diversity at the Azusa Street Mission, the cultural component is evident. "The closing years of the eighteenth and the early decades of the nineteenth centuries witnessed an unprecedented spread of Christianity among Afro-Americans, slave and free."[217] The Jim Crow laws succeeded in segregating the worshippers of God. According to Kennedy, within the segregated territories, you could count on one hand the number of white churches that would allow blacks into their sanctuaries to worship.[218] One only has to look to history to see why "the most segregated hour of Christian America is eleven o'clock on Sunday morning."[219] The influence and guidelines of the Jim Crow laws molded a generation, presenting racism as a norm to some and inferiority as a norm to others. The dilemma of blacks from the South was described in this way: "Forgotten in the North, manipulated and the callously rejected by the South, rebuffed by the Supreme Court, voiceless in national affairs, he and his descendants were condemned in the interests of sectional harmony to lives of poverty, indignity, and little hope."[220]

---

216 Randolph, "Plantation Churches," 67.
217 Raboteau, *Slave Religion*, 152.
218 Kennedy, *Jim Crow Guide*, 197.
219 Days before his assassination on March 31, 1968, Martin Luther King preached these words at the National Cathedral in Washington, DC.
220 John A. Garraty, *The American Nation to 1877: A History of the United States* (New York: Harper and Row, 1963), 447.

Three
Relationship and Conflict

Some authors have hailed the initial meeting between Seymour and Parham as the monumental step toward the Pentecostal movement, but one author speculated that "Parham planted the seed, but Seymour gave birth and later nurturing to the experience of Pentecostalism."[221] Whether or not either statement is factual, the movement came by way of relationship and conflict in the Jim Crow era. The Jim Crow period "was, at its core, a structure of exclusion and discrimination devised by white Americans to be employed principally against black Americans—though others felt its sting as well, not least Hispanics and Asians, and even whites who opposed it."[222] Seymour, who was an African American, and Parham, who was a white man, were on opposite sides of this racial divide. Both men were bent on doing what they presumed to be God's will, even if it meant challenging church doctrines that were commonly accepted by the populace. Ultimately for these two men, sharing particular doctrines would prove to be disadvantageous.

Seymour attended a church in Houston led by a black woman by the name of Lucy F. Farrow, a widow with seven children. Farrow was sold into slavery at birth in 1851 in Norfolk, Virginia. Farrow was also the niece of

---

221 Sanders, *William Joseph Seymour*, 5.
222 Packard, *American Nightmare*, vi.

Frederick Douglass,[223] a notable African American abolitionist. She pastored a small holiness church while working as a nanny, cook, and governess. "William, who was well-liked by Pastor Farrow and the congregation, would eventually become the interim pastor of the small church when Pastor Farrow would go to Kansas to work as a 'governess' in the home of Rev. Charles Fox Parham."[224] She also served as a cook for Parham when he and his workers would travel to Houston to hold meetings. According to Robeck, Farrow's employment as a cook for Parham's organization was due to her being a light-skinned woman.[225] Employment of light-skinned blacks in the homes and organizations of whites was not uncommon during the Jim Crow era. In fact, many "light-skinned blacks during the Jim Crow era sometimes cut off relations from friends and family in an effort to 'pass' as white and enjoy the upward mobility and privilege associated with whiteness."[226]

Farrow was very attentive to the teachings of Parham, especially his doctrine of the baptism of the Holy Spirit. "A benefit of her short-term employment was attending Parham's services and thoroughly indoctrinating herself in Pentecostal theology."[227] It was there that she received the baptism of the Holy Spirit and spoke in tongues. Farrow returned to Houston with the Parham family, proposing to bring her church under the umbrella of Parham's Apostolic Faith Movement. She enlightened Seymour about her experience of being baptized in the Holy Spirit and speaking in tongues. Seymour, like numerous other holiness people, believed that one receives the Holy Spirit at the time of sanctification. During Seymour's time in Jackson, Mississippi, he had been under the

---

223 Frederick Douglass (1818–1995) was "an American slave, was an abolitionist, women's rights advocate, journalist and newspaper editor, social reformer and race leader." John Hunt, *The Essential Writings of the American Black Church* (Chattanooga, TN: AMG Publishers, 2008), 380.
224 Sanders, *William Joseph Seymour*, 59.
225 Robeck Jr., *The Azusa Street Mission and Revival*, 44.
226 Michelle Alexander, *The New Jim Crow: Mass Incarceration in the Age of Colorblindness* (New York: The New Press, 2010), 162.
227 Goff Jr., *Fields White unto Harvest*, 107.

spiritual advisement of Charles P. Jones,[228] who taught him that the holiness doctrine of sanctification was "that act of Divine grace whereby we are made holy in justification, the guilt of sin is removed. Sanctification must be definitely experienced to fit us to see the Lord."[229] Therefore, Seymour was somewhat resistant to Farrow's newfound teaching.[230] News of Parham opening a Bible school in Houston piqued Seymour's interest. The Jim Crow laws, however, explicitly forbade the mixing of races in most settings, and classrooms were no exception. Following the introduction of Seymour to Parham, which was prompted by Farrow, Seymour eventually enrolled in Parham's Bible school, which consisted of training sessions, which lasted ten weeks and covered such topics as repentance, conversion, conviction, sanctification, consecration, and healing.

The school was held in Bryan Hall, an old building on the corner of Rusk Street and Brazos Street. Despite his strained financial situation, Parham did not charge students for attending. The students were taught to rely on faith, and Parham relied on the donations of Pentecostal devotees to cover many of the school's expenses.[231] Parham made it clear that the Bible school was run like the military, with set hours to rise, sleep, study, and eat. He had an arduous schedule in place at the school. A student named Howard Goss recalls this of his time spent in Parham's school: "We were given a thorough workout and a rigid training in prayer, fasting, consecration, Bible study and evangelistic work. Our week day schedule consisted of Bible study in the morning, shop and jail meetings at noon, house to house visitations in the afternoon, and six o'clock street meeting followed by an evangelistic service at seven or eight o'clock."[232]

---

228 Charles P. Jones was raised as a Baptist. He graduated from Arkansas Baptist College and pastored several Baptist churches in Arkansas, Alabama, and Mississippi. Martin, *The Life and Ministry of William J. Seymour*, 87.
229 J. Gordon Melton, *The Encyclopedia of American Religions: Religious Creeds* (Detroit: Gale Research Inc., 1994), 321.
230 Martin, *The Life and Ministry of William J. Seymour*, 90.
231 Goff Jr., *Fields White unto Harvest*, 106. The operational budget for Parham's Bible school was about one hundred dollars per week.
232 Bernard Broussard tells this story in *A History of St. Mary Parish* (unpublished manuscript, 1955).

Parham's dedication to his calling was enthusiastically displayed in the evening when he and his students would dress up in impressive Holy Land apparel and march down Main Street, holding a sizeable banner with the words "Apostolic Faith Movement" printed on it. Parham was a teacher by day and a street evangelist by night. These marches preceded a nightly service held at Bryan Hall. Parham's notoriety as a "divine healer" came in handy for the students, as Parham would make himself available for two hours each day to pray for the sick. [233]

Seymour's admittance into Parham's school was described by one scholar as Parham's "most important decision at the Houston school, considering the late history of Pentecostalism."[234] Seymour's admittance, particularly his seating arrangements and Parham's position on race relations, has been explored and debated by several authors. Local Jim Crow laws prohibited integrated schooling at the time, but Parham's unending fervor to extend the Pentecostal dogma to the masses—particularly the African American community—impelled him to make an exception to the rule and allow Seymour to enroll in the Bible college. Whether seated in an adjoining room, sitting in a hallway within earshot of an open door, or seated in a chair outside of an open window, Seymour's thirst for knowledge was quenched by Parham's theology. Concerning Seymour's admittance to the school, one thing remains clear: the laws in place at that time would have not permitted him to sit among white classmates. Although Seymour was not allowed to interact with the white students, he became so immersed in his studies that he was able to recite Parham's teachings from memory.[235]

3.1 CAROTHERS

A man by the name of Warren Faye Carothers played a vital role in the relationship between Seymour and Parham. Carothers was an "attorney, judge, pastor, denominational executive, ecumenist."[236] In 1905, while

---
233 Robeck Jr., *The Azusa Street Mission and Revival*, 46.
234 Goff Jr., *Fields White unto Harvest*, 107.
235 Martin, *The Life and Ministry of William J. Seymour*, 93.
236 C. M. Robeck Jr., "Warren Fay Carothers," in *Dictionary of Pentecostal and Charismatic Movements*, ed. Stanley M. Burgess, Gary B. McGee, and Patrick H.

pastoring a holiness church in Brunner, Texas, Carothers met Parham during Parham's move to Houston. One year later, after merging his flock with Parham's ministry and embracing the Apostolic Faith Movement (AFM), Carothers added a new position to his long list of accomplishments. He became Parham's field director and chief lieutenant of Texas. His oratory skills and association with the press earned him a position as the spokesperson and advocate for Houston. Carothers's duties included the training of pastors and evangelists and the selection of other directors, and he also oversaw the annual AFM conventions. In fact, Carothers would later award Seymour his credentials and authorize his move to Los Angeles.[237] "In March 1906 W. F. Carothers outlined his own racial ideology. His ardent segregation policy extended far beyond Parham's explanation of superior and inferior races."[238]

Whereas Parham detested interracial marriages, Carothers forbade any kind of contact between blacks and whites, social or otherwise: "He happened upon the novel interpretation that racial animosity was a corrective gift from God to ensure separation."[239]

Carothers stated, "Now to meet this unnatural, unheard of condition, God has resorted to the next best expedient, and through His spirit has intensified the racial impulses between the white and black man as the only remaining possible barrier to the miscegenation of their respective races. This intensified racial impulse is mistaken by many outsiders for prejudice, or a work of the devil, when in truth it is the work of the Holy Spirit, and such is binding upon all Christians."[240] Borlase states, "Parham was liberal compared to fellow member of the Apostolic Faith W. F. Carothers."[241] They both, however, shared the view of "white, Anglo-Saxon Protestants as in some way especially blessed by God, a superior

---

Alexander (Grand Rapids: Zondervan Publishing House, 1988), 108.
237 Ibid.
238 Goff Jr., *Fields White unto Harvest*, 108.
239 Ibid.
240 Goff Jr., *Fields White unto Harvest*, 109.
241 Borlase, *William Seymour: A Biography*, 83.

people, and this inevitably placed African Americans and other people of color at a distinct disadvantage."[242]

Parham leaned on Carothers for ingenuity, and Carothers's knowledge of the Houston area came in handy, allowing Parham and Carothers to take the gospel into the community. Yet "Carothers's ideal was a Pentecostal revival which spread from white to white and black to black."[243] Seymour was the likely candidate to take the apostolic message to the black areas of the city since Parham and Carothers had taught him the Pentecostal doctrine. Seymour was also given an opportunity that was not often afforded to blacks in that time. He was given the chance to preach "at least once at the Brunner Tabernacle, under the watchful eyes of its pastor, Warren Faye Carothers, and his teacher, Charles Parham."[244] Letters later written by Carothers revealed his plans to evangelize the black communities of Texas: "Inherent in the plan was the assumption that white leaders would train black leaders, a la Seymour, and that blacks would follow proper social etiquette when interacting with their white Pentecostals."[245] This was nothing new; this pattern began in the late eighteenth century. White ministers observed that slaves were more receptive to their own kind as preachers. In 1863, a white minister stated this: "The colored brethren are so much preferred as *preachers*. When in the pulpit there is a wonderful sympathy between the speaker and his audience. This sympathetic influence seems the result of a…peculiar experience. None but a Negro can so preach as fully to arouse, excite, and transport a Negro".[246]

Much like the watchful eyes fixed on Seymour, the slave owners ensured that the slave preachers were constantly supervised. "Carefully watched and viewed with suspicion, the preacher had to straddle the conflict between the demands of conscience and the orders of the

---

242 Robeck Jr., *The Azusa Street Mission and Revival*, 48.
243 Goff Jr., *Fields White unto Harvest*, 109.
244 Robeck Jr., *The Azusa Street Mission and Revival*, 49.
245 Goff Jr., *Fields White unto Harvest*, 109.
246 Raboteau, *Slave Religion*, 234–235.

master."247 Despite Seymour's glowing reviews from his colleagues—both white and black—he was not exempt from condemnation if he stepped across the doctrinal line that was put in place by his spiritual leaders. Later, after witnessing ceaseless partiality against his fellow black Christians, Seymour came to believe in "the dissolution of racial barriers that was the surest sign of the Spirit's Pentecostal presence and the approaching Jerusalem."248 This, of course, ran contrary to Parham's theory, which insisted that tongues were the unquestionable sign of the baptism of the Holy Spirit. On the other hand, Carothers answered both by openly declaring "that it was racial hatred, not tongues, that was a true gift of the Spirit."249 Aside from Parham and Carothers—who had left Seymour prior to his new theory—numerous brothers in the faith deserted Seymour. His woes seemed so reminiscent of those who were before him. According to Raboteau, "The slave preacher who verged too close on a gospel of equality within earshot of whites was in trouble."250

According to Borlase, "The period that closed 1905 and opened 1906 would be the time when Seymour and Parham were at their closest. They spent more time together than at any other time, and their friendship would never again have such currency."251 While many of Parham's teachings concerning the historical aspects of scripture—such as the creation account and the flood account—were prejudiced against blacks, he made a concerted effort to share the Pentecostal message with them.252 Goff insists, "He felt a special obligation to those races he considered inferior."253 Seymour and Parham's closeness was seen in the midst of segregated crowds in the black neighborhoods—they stood by each other, proclaiming the gospel.

---

247 Ibid., 232.
248 Cox, *Fire from Heaven*, 63.
249 Borlase, *William Seymour: A Biography*, 178.
250 Raboteau, *Slave Religion*, 232.
251 Borlase, *William Seymour*, 81.
252 See chapter 4 on *"Raceology"*
253 Goff Jr., *Fields White unto Harvest*, 107.

Parham's eagerness to reach out to the black districts of Houston can be viewed as a sure sign of his belief that the Pentecostal message was for all races. There was, however, no indication that this altered his beliefs about segregation. Whereas some labeled Parham's efforts as a form of cloaked racism, Goff offers a much more generous description of Parham's outreach efforts: "Parham occupied a paternalistic middle ground typical of many if not most white ministers from the Midwest."[254] Goff later asserts, "Parham's sensitivity to black people's needs would decrease with age and in response to his bitter break with Seymour and Azusa Street."[255]

---

254 Ibid.,111.
255 Ibid.,110.

Four
"Raceology"

Some of the conflict surrounding Seymour, Parham, and the Pentecostal movement could possibly be attributed to theology and race. Regarding Pentecostal theology, Jacobsen claims this: "Race is an essential part of the equation because, from the very beginning, Pentecostalism straddled the race line in ways that most other American religious movements did not."[256] Neither white nor black could lay total claim to the movement; in essence, the movement belonged to all ethnicities. The Azusa Street Mission gave evidence that the Holy Spirit showed no partiality. A rabbi and a reporter for the *Los Angeles Times* attended a meeting on Tuesday, April 17, 1906. The rabbi unexpectedly converted. The journalist, however, "could not decide what to be more astounded by—the sense of something powerful yet invisible rampaging throughout the room or the sight of black and white leaning on, praying for, and weeping, laughing, and rejoicing with each other."[257] Prior to Seymour's newfound theology, which he had acquired from Parham, Seymour's conversion took place in Indianapolis at Simpson Chapel Methodist Episcopal Church. Although the church had a predominately black congregation, the message of integration and unity was regularly preached. According to Martin, "As the Methodists drifted toward the left, many conservative members left

---

256 Jacobsen, *Thinking in the Spirit*, 260.
257 Borlase, *William Seymour*, 126.

their ranks, starting a national holiness movement."[258] Seymour felt that he had overstayed his welcome when the Methodists rejected his doctrine of premillennialism.[259] Raised as a Baptist with a Catholic influence, Seymour's doctrinal views were collected in fragments over time during his spiritual journey. "He held tight to certain key doctrines, primarily believing that above all things, faith was the key."[260] Seymour's doctrine of premillennialism as well as his fascination with "special revelation" were readily accepted by and were in step with the teachings of his former teacher Martin Knapp.

Knapp's rendition of special revelation had a much different connotation from what Seymour had been exposed to in the black community in Louisiana: "There are many slave narratives going back to the 18th century, in which slaves talked about receiving guidance through visions and dreams, hearing voices, and experiencing different states of altered consciousness such as trances. All of this suggests that the role of what might be called 'special revelation' was widely accepted within the African American community."[261]

It was known that this type of special revelation was not reserved for Christian believers only; it also occurred in African American traditional folk magic called "voodoo." Knapp, however, insisted one must take visions, dreams, and internal voices seriously. He warned that one must discern the spirits to recognize which manifestations came from God.[262] Knapp's interpretation of special revelation, racial inclusiveness, and sanctification sat well with Seymour. Rufus G.W. Sanders says that the holiness ministry of the Cincinnati preacher Martin Wells Knapp changed Seymour's

---

258 Martin, *The Life and Ministry of William J. Seymour*, 72.
259 "Premillennialists believe in a literal return of the Lord before a literal period of one thousand years [millennium] during which He will rule over the earth." Robeck Jr., *The Azusa Street Mission and Revival*, 29. "Whereas, 'amillennial' a position held by the Methodist, in which millennium is viewed as a figurative or spiritual reality and not a literal reality to which the return of the Lord might be tied" Ibid., 29.
260 Borlase, *William Seymour*, 49.
261 Robeck Jr., *The Azusa Street Mission and Revival*, 33.
262 Ibid, 34.

life forever.[263] In fact, Knapp's description of the church was mirrored at Azusa Street: "There can be neither Jew nor Greek…Barriers of race and color, and social position have no true place in Christ's church. High toned social clubs, claiming to be churches, but throwing stones of criticism and ostracism at saints of God because of cast color, are among the most stupendous of Satan's frauds which curse the earth today…Respecters and selectors of persons…What a contrast to the 'Body of Christ.'"[264]

In 1902, after a long refusal to accept his call to ministry, Seymour finally relented and became "a follower of William Wells Knapp and his doctrine of holiness. William made a spiritual commitment to become a minister of the Gospel."[265] Seymour's pilgrimage to Houston tested many of his beliefs. Knapp and his followers denounced Parham's theology—particularly speaking in tongues. "An article in *The Gospel Trumpet*, official organ for the Saints, ridiculed the group's tongue speaking, saying students at Topeka 'chattered an incomprehensible jargon.'"[266]

Seymour eventually adhered to Parham's view that the baptism of the Holy Spirit was the third work of grace and that speaking in tongues was the prerequisite. Seymour continued to reject "the existing racial barriers in favor of 'unity in Christ.' He also rejected the then almost-universal barriers to women in any form of church leadership."[267] The mixing of racism and theology is seen throughout Parham's doctrinal views. Seymour may have embraced some of the basic elements of Parham's doctrines[268] initially—such as "Parham's concern for evangelization, his emphasis upon sanctification and the pursuit of holiness, his teaching on the baptism in the Spirit with the Bible evidence of speaking in other tongues, his emphasis upon

---

263 Sanders, *William J. Seymour*, 52.
264 Ibid., 53
265 Ibid., 54
266 Martin, *The Life and Ministry of William J. Seymour*, 90-91; Jennie C. Rutty, "The Gift of Tongues," *The Gospel Trumpet* (1902), 3.
267 Hunt, ed., The Essential Writings of the American Black Church, 708.
268 "Parham himself preferred the term Apostolic Faith as the best way of referring to his views and the movement he was trying to foster." D. William Faupel, *The Everlasting Gospel: The Significance of Eschatology in the Development of Pentecostal Thought* (Sheffield, England: Sheffield Academic Press, 1996), 167–168.

divine healing, and his premillennial position on the second coming."[269] However, Seymour became troubled by some of Parham's more extreme teachings—such as his teaching of the annihilation of the wicked,[270] his belief that the flood was caused by interracial marriage,[271] and his doctrine of "Anglo-Israelism," which contends that Anglo-Saxons are the ten lost tribes of Israel.[272] Seymour ardently rejected these doctrines. However, despite the numerous negative reports and documentations of Parham's beliefs, doctrines, and suspicious associations, some authors have denied the validity of these reports. According to Walter Hollenwegger, "Parham's pacifism, his doctrine on the 'destruction of the wicked,' his animosity to medicine, his 'Anglo-Israel' theories, his sympathy with the Ku Klux Klan—all this has been contradicted by Pentecostalism."[273] According to Jacobsen, "Parham was far from being a typical American theologian."[274] He insists that Parham "was clearly idiosyncratic in many of his views."[275] To comprehend the theological mindset of Parham, one must be familiar with his foundation. Like Seymour, Parham also had a bout with a deadly illness called rheumatic fever, which haunted him from childhood. Also like Seymour, Parham viewed his illness as a call from God. Parham relished the fact that his religious education as a child was deficient because it allowed him to read the Bible without any partialities.

Parham began attending Southwest Kansas College in 1890, but he later said that his three-year stint was a hindrance to him. Parham felt that his school studies conflicted with his call to preach.[276] Eventually he

---

269 Robeck Jr., *The Azusa Street Mission and Revival*, 50.
270 Charles F. Parham, *The Everlasting Gospel* (Baxter Springs, KS: Apostolic Faith Bible College), 111–117.
271 Charles F. Parham, "God's Plan of the Ages," *Gospel of the Kingdom* (1910), 1.
272 Charles F. Parham, *Kol Kare Bomidbar: A Voice Crying in the Wilderness* (Baxter Springs, KS: Apostolic Faith Bible College), 105–108.
273 Walter J. Hollenweger, "*Pentecostalism: Origins and Developments Worldwide* (Peabody, MA: Hendrickson Publishers, 1997), 23.
274 Jacobsen, *Thinking in the Spirit*, 19.
275 Ibid.
276 Parham began his studies to prepare for the Methodist ministry, and according to Goff, "Money became important to Parham." He decided to change his studies in

decided to abandon college and sought out a pastorate at a Methodist church in Eudora in 1893. Two years later, he decided to leave the Methodist church. "His strict religious devotion had led him to be much impressed by the holiness movement,"[277] which was taking form at that time. One of Parham's major influences at that time was a man named David Baker, a holiness-oriented Quaker. Baker was the driving force behind Parham's new outlook on the Christian faith, and he was especially enamored with the movement's commitment. In 1895, Parham decided to start his own ministry. "Parham's overriding concern was to connect spiritually with people's practical needs, and to that end he added a range of new initiatives to the mission's program of ministries, including an orphanage, a rescue mission aimed at the town's prostitutes, a soup kitchen, and a shelter for the homeless."[278]

"Parham was the first person to formulate the Pentecostal doctrine of necessary, or evidential, tongues—that is, the assertion that speaking in tongues must be a part of any experience of the Baptism of the Holy Spirit for it to be deemed genuine."[279] Parham believed that speaking in tongues was in fact a foreign language, enabling those who received this gift to speak to others in their native languages. "For Parham, the immediacy of revelation was always central to his thinking."[280]

Parham's take on the book of Genesis looks very unconventional in comparison to numerous renderings from other interpreters. Parham

---

pursuit of a medical career. Eventually his spiritual fervor subsided, leaving him in a "backslidden" state. He was soon after struck with rheumatic fever, which he felt was brought on by God. The pain was so severe that he had trouble walking. Later, after returning from a long stint of bed rest, his ankles were too weak to support him, causing him to hobble around campus. In December 1891 while sitting "under an old oak tree on the college lawn, he renewed his vow to preach the Gospel and promised to quit college if that was what God wanted. In that moment of dedication, he found his ankles instantly healed." He continued school for two more terms while ministering, and it was at this point that school apparently became a distraction from his love of preaching. Goff Jr., *Fields White unto Harvest*, 29.
277 Ibid., 33.
278 Jacobsen, *Thinking in the Spirit*, 23.
279 Jacobsen, *Thinking in the Spirit*, 19.
280 Bearman and Mills, "Charles M. Sheldon and Charles F. Parham," 119.

began by insisting that not only were Adam and Eve driven out of Eden, but they were also made to reside with an inferior race. He goes on to speculate that Cain, after murdering his brother Abel, took a wife from his newfound home among the first race (inferior first creation). The interracial marriage of Cain infuriated God so much that He caused a flood to obliterate what Parham calls the "unsouled people" and those who chose to intermingle with them.[281] The following is an excerpt from Parham's sermon titled "Creation and Formation": "Thus began the woeful intermarriage of races for which cause the flood was sent in punishment, and has never been followed by plagues and incurable diseases upon the third and fourth generations, the offspring of such marriages. Were time to last and intermarriage continue between the whites, the blacks and the reds of America, consumption and other disease would soon wipe the mixed bloods off the face of the earth."[282]

According to Goff, "Parham interjected a dose of racial ideology that many of his hearers no doubt instinctively applauded."[283] Parham stood firm in the Anglo-Saxon position, remaining consistent in his dispensing of racial hypotheses: "The Old Testament distinction of the peoples of the earth remains almost the same today. The Hebrew, Jews and the various descendants of the ten tribes—the Anglo-Saxons, High Germans, Danes (Dan), Swedes, Hindoos, Japanese and the Hindoo-Japanese of Hawaii, and these possess about all the spiritual power of the world. The Gentiles—French, Spanish, Italian, Greek, Russian and Turkish. These are formalistic, and so are their descendants in all parts of the world. Heathen are mostly heathen still—the Negro, Malay, Mongolian and Indian."[284]

Parham was also more than certain that the ark of the covenant held some significant source of power, which would benefit the Jewish efforts to return to their homeland. According to Goff, "Parham announced that

---

281 Goff Jr., *Fields White unto Harvest*, 103.
282 Ibid., 104; see also "Creation and Formation," *Houston Daily Post*, August 13, 1905.
283 Goff Jr., *Fields White unto Harvest*, 104.
284 *Apostolic Faith* 1 (1899): 4.

he had discovered a secret tip about the Ark's whereabouts in an old Jewish document."[285] Parham's theology was very peculiar. Without any formal theological training, Parham relied on his own interpretive skills to decipher the Christian message. In fact, Parham was very vocal about his disdain for those who attended seminaries to acquire credentials. He once said, "The title DD, or Doctor of Divinity, stood for 'dumb dogs' and that 'seminaries' should be spelled and pronounced 'cemeteries.'"[286] He maintained these views while discounting the ancient creeds of Christendom. "At one point, Parham called those creeds nothing but 'the sawdust of men's opinions.' And he felt no need for his own theology to be bound by them."[287] In *A Voice Crying in the Wilderness*, Parham depicts the church and education as the adversaries of those seeking to fulfill God's will:

> Most sectarian schools afford the best facilities for back-sliding, the religious influence being often dominated by back-slidden, super-annuated preachers; who, if they are not back-slidden before, are in great danger of it after being superannuated and located in the College town of their denomination; for many of them are not willing to live a quiet and peaceful life, but having been in the habit of having their own way so long, seek to rule the affairs of the Church and College upon old and prosaic lines, and are soon outclassed by younger men of more progressive, and in many cases, deeper spiritual truths.[288]

Much of what is highlighted in the literary works about Parham and his contributions to Pentecostalism is speaking in tongues or the "second blessing." "Parham and his followers concluded that speaking in tongues

---

285 Goff Jr., *Fields White unto Harvest*, 102.
286 Bearman and Mills, "Charles M. Sheldon and Charles F. Parham," 116; Ferenc Morton Szasz, *Religion in the Modern American West* (Tucson: University of Arizona Press, 2000), 83; Parham, *A Voice Crying in the Wilderness*, 11–20.
287 Jacobsen, *Thinking in the Spirit*, 19.
288 Parham, *A Voice Crying in the Wilderness*, 11.

and the baptism of the Holy Ghost were inseparable. They developed the position that speaking in tongues was the audible signal that God was with them and that this speech served as an empowering tool for evangelism."[289] Parham labeled this sign the "second blessing," and he ardently encouraged others to seek it. Seymour also adopted Parham's doctrine of the second blessing, believing that speaking in tongues was the evidence of the baptism of the Holy Spirit. However, Seymour's acceptance of the doctrine came long before he actually received the experience. The perceived way of seeking the baptism of the Holy Ghost at the time was tarrying at the altar. In Seymour's case, the altar was at Parham's meeting. Unfortunately, Seymour was unable to seek the baptism there due to Parham's policy, which forbade blacks and whites from integrating at the altar. "Whites were given the primary seats in the auditorium or sanctuary, while African Americans were required to sit or stand in the rear."[290] Yet it would be unfair to place all the blame on Parham because the racial system in that time, known as Jim Crow, enforced segregation in all facilities, and the church was no exception. Whether or not the Jim Crow laws were a hindrance to white ministers who truly wanted to desegregate worship or a form of support for those who detested desegregation, the Jim Crow laws had to be upheld.[291]

In regard to the church and prejudice, Fredrick Douglass gave an address at the Plymouth County Anti-Slavery Society on November 4, 1841:

> At the South I was a member of the Methodist Church. When I came north, I thought one Sunday I would attend communion, at one of the churches of my denomination, in the town I was staying. The white people gathered round the altar, the blacks clustered by the door. After the good minister had served out the bread

---
289 Bearman and Mills, "Charles M. Sheldon and Charles F. Parham," 118.
290 Robeck Jr., *The Azusa Street Mission and Revival*, 46–47.
291 Prior to the initiation of the Jim Crow laws, many white ministers had already put similar rules in place.

and wine to one portion of those near him, he said, "These may withdraw, and others come forward;" thus he proceeded till all the white members had been served. Then he took a long breath, and looking out toward the door, exclaimed, "Come up, colored friends, come up! For you know God is no respecter of persons!" I haven't been there to see the sacraments taken since.[292]

Despite the order of laws and practices that were set in place, Seymour remained fervent in his quest for the second blessing. His pursuit was ongoing. It was not until April 12, 1906, that Seymour would receive the experience of speaking in tongues. A doctrine that Seymour at one time questioned eventually became the magnum opus of his ministry. Ironically, "Seymour and a white brother had tarried late, seeking the Holy Spirit."[293] After receiving the baptism and speaking in tongues, "he testified that it was like a sphere of fiery, white-hot radiance falling upon him."[294] His devotion to Parham's theology of speaking in tongues would later be understood as the initial spark that ignited the fire at the Azusa Street Mission.

---

292 Frederick Douglass, "The Church and Prejudice," in *The Essential Writings of the American Black Church*, ed. John Hunt (Chattanooga, TN: AMG Publishers, 2008), 397.
293 Martin, *The Life and Ministry of William J. Seymour*, 148.
294 Ibid.

Five

Seymour and Parham Reunited

Seymour's train ride of 1,371 miles from Houston to Los Angeles in January of 1906 contained many tests and trials. The Jim Crow laws restricted the traveling accommodations for black people. Blacks were "barred from taking up a place in either of the first two classes of carriage. That meant no sleeper, no space, and minimal chance of relaxation."[295] This ban would spread to the third-class carriages if whites needed more space, leaving the black passengers in the aisle or riding with the freight. Clergymen were entitled to certain privileges when traveling during this time, but according to Borlase, none of these privileges were extended to Seymour.[296]

Seymour's journey to Azusa Street was met with some antagonism along the way. On his trek to Los Angeles, Seymour was afforded the opportunity to stop and lodge at one of Alma White's homes in Colorado.[297] Alma White was an ardent opponent of the Pentecostal movement, and she made her revulsion for Seymour known. Once he arrived in Los Angeles, he met Julia Hutchins, the catalyst of his relocating to Los Angeles. She later became discontent with his doctrinal views

---

295 Borlase, *William Seymour*, 88.
296 Ibid.
297 Alma White's home was a part of "a network of nineteen houses countrywide that offered free accommodations to the traveling men of the cloth." Borlase, *William Seymour*, 88.

and locked him out of the church where he was to become a pastor. He found himself hosting large revivals in a home on Bonnie Brae Avenue, and ultimately, Seymour and his newfound followers ended up at an unsightly abandoned warehouse and livery stable with a dirt floor at 312 Azusa Street. Harvey Cox states, "They swept it out and moved their daily meetings there on April 14, 1906. It was no White City, but from that nondescript storehouse where on a rainy day one could still detect the scent of horses, a spiritual fire roared forth that was to race around the world and touch hundreds of millions of people with its warmth and power."[298]

Not only did the congregation grow at Azusa Street, the criticism of Seymour and his spiritual movement also increased. "Many felt that the meetings were becoming nothing but side shows of devil-inspired emotionalism. Some felt the services were too extreme even for traditional holiness people."[299] Seymour tried to tame the emotional outbursts by toning down his rhetoric about speaking in tongues. His attempt, however, failed. According to Frank Bartleman, the Azusa phenomenon was seen as God working powerfully in all who attended the meetings. Bartleman notes that despite persecution from the press, which proved to be a great boost rather than a deterrent for attendance, "It seemed that everyone had to go to Azusa. Missionaries were gathered there from Africa, India, and the islands of the sea. Preachers and workers had crossed the continent and come from distant lands with an irresistible drawing to Los Angeles."[300]

Much can be said about Seymour's leadership at Azusa. He was a blind-in-one-eye exhorter. He was caught up in an unexpected whirlwind of the Holy Spirit, and he was also witnessing the transformation of a segregated people into a united people. "What was happening at Azusa Street was new. There were no books that gave instructions on how to establish a Pentecostal church or how to lead and disciple Pentecostal

---

298 Cox, *Fire from Heaven*, 46.
299 Sanders, *William Joseph Seymour*, 100.
300 Bartleman, *Azusa Street*, 50

believers."[301] His limited education, however, had no effect on his limitless study of scripture, which led him to select the passages for his instruction. These passages were Acts; 1 Corinthians 12–14; Romans 12:1–8; Ephesians 4:1–16; and 1 Peter 4:7–11.[302]

Pastoral instruction from the surrounding clergy in Los Angeles was unattainable, seeing as their doctrinal stances differed from Seymour's. Only one man could fill that instructional chasm. "Exhilarated by the wonderful fruits of his ministry, Seymour had invited his former teacher [Parham] to come and see for himself if indeed the outpouring of blessing before the end time had not in fact begun."[303] Those who were close to Seymour were also anxious for Parham's arrival; in fact, "one remarked that he wanted to see the white 'father of the black son.'"[304] Everyone was certain that Parham's presence would bring a sense of validation to the Azusa Street Mission: "Parham was recognized, not only by Seymour but the entire Pentecostal movement, as a man of wisdom and experience."[305]

Parham's arrival in late October was not a pleasant one. The sounds of "ostentatious shouts and jabberings" caught Parham's ear before he entered the door of the Azusa Street Mission. This so incensed Parham that he wasted no time and began admonishing the congregation. He made his way to the front of the church and began his rant against what he saw as an abomination. According to Martin, Parham greeted Seymour before proclaiming God's displeasure in the activities at Azusa.[306]

Although one could readily find fault with Parham's conduct, there are particular factors that impacted Parham's response that must be examined. Some have written that in October 1906, Seymour invited Parham to lead a union revival. Goff states, "Parham later claimed that

---

301 Robeck Jr., *The Azusa Street Mission & Revival*, 110.
302 Ibid.
303 Cox, *Fire from Heaven*, 60.
304 Martin, *The Life and Ministry of William J. Seymour*, 268.
305 Sanders, *William Joseph Seymour*, 108.
306 Martin, *The Life and Ministry of William J. Seymour*, 269; Borlase, *William Seymour*, 165.

Seymour's letters had urged his arrival specifically 'to help him discern between that which was real and that which was false.'"[307] The latter appeared to be what Parham thought he was encountering when entering the Azusa Street Mission. One may conclude that Parham's criticizing of Azusa was in fact a result of his discernment. Nevertheless, "the congregation was as unhappy with Parham as he was with them."[308] Very little can be found about Seymour's disposition during this turn of events or about any conversation between him and Parham. According to Sanders, "Parham tried to persuade Seymour to resign and turn the reins over to him."[309] Seymour's answer appeared to be evident when the name "The Apostolic Faith Movement of Los Angeles" was soon changed to "The Pacific Apostolic Faith Movement, Head Quarters, Los Angeles."[310] This was a clear indication that the Azusa Street Mission was now reidentifying itself. The spewing of racial epithets later surfaced in Parham's publications in regard to Azusa as well as in his countless references to demonic possession and spirits,[311] leaving some to speculate about his true intentions regarding Seymour. Borlase insists, "On so many levels it was inevitable that he would disapprove—Parham was at the peak of his prestige, yet here was a former pupil creating a monumental stir without him. Parham had spearheaded the drive toward tongues and baptism in the Spirit: Seymour was simply borrowing the script. Finally, Parham was white; Seymour was black."[312]

"While scholars such as Kenyon, Tinney, and Lovett believe Parham's racism was evident throughout his ministry, Goff asserted that Parham experienced a transformation 'Not unlike Tom Watson's switch from Populist Libertarian to racist demagogue' after his experience at Azusa

---

307 Goff Jr., *Fields White unto Harvest*, 130.
308 Martin, *The Life and Ministry of William J. Seymour*, 270.
309 Sanders, *William Joseph Seymour*, 109.
310 Nelson, For Such a Time as This, 211.
311 Cox, *Fire from Heaven*, 61;Robeck Jr., *The Azusa Street Mission & Revival*, 169; Sanders, *William Joseph Seymour*, 108.
312 Borlase, *William Seymour*, 164.

Street in 1906."[313] The severing of Seymour and Parham's relationship was inevitable. Despite the criticism from Seymour's former tutor, "the Azusa Street revival itself continued day after day, month after month for three years."[314] Anticipations and hopes of unanimity were shattered, but the Azusa Street Mission was not. "While *The Apostolic Faith* had been full of the news of Parham's visit in the issues published in the two months leading up to it, once he touched down there was nothing more said."[315] It later became apparent that "Parham's authority was undermined by the phenomenal growth of the movement."[316] None other than Parham's comrade, Carothers, who "insisted that if Seymour had appealed the matter to the entire Apostolic Faith body, 'we would have remained united, because the older part of the movement approved the action which he thought we would condemn,'" called Parham's abrupt dismissal of the events at Azusa into question.[317] In 1908, Carothers wrote that the Azusa revival was "one of the greatest revivals of modern times."[318]

---

313 Joe Newman, *Race and the Assemblies of God Church: The Journey from Azusa Street to the "Miracle of Memphis"* (Youngstown, New York: Cambria Press, 2007), footnote. See also Goff Jr., *Fields White unto Harvest*, 235; C. Vann Woodward, *Tom Watson: Agrarian Rebel* (New York: Oxford Press, 1963); and David Chalmers, *Hooded Americanism: The History of the Ku Klux Klan* (New York: New Viewpoints, 1981).
314 Cox, *Fire from Heaven*, 46.
315 Borlase, *William Seymour*, 165.
316 Goff Jr., *Fields White unto Harvest*, 142.
317 Ibid; *Herald of the Church* 1 (1925): 10–11.
318 Goff Jr., *Fields White unto Harvest*, 142.

Six
Conclusion

Much of what is known about the relationship between William Seymour and Charles Parham has been documented in autobiographies, encyclopedias of Christian-history, articles, and periodicals. The methodologies of the writers differ according to their interests in or relationships to the individuals and the Pentecostal movement. Whether they are condemning or commending the movement impacts their research. The prevailing argument in regard to Seymour and Parham's relationship hinges on racism and in some cases, Parham's envy.[319] Many have come to Parham's defense in this matter; others continue to hold fast to their negative perception of Parham.

All of the information found or compiled about William Seymour paints him as meek or compliant. In fact, throughout Parham's visit, Seymour was able to maintain his tranquil demeanor. Taking into consideration the whites who would frequent Seymour's church on occasion, one could argue that because of the Jim Crow laws that were in place at the time, it was virtually impossible for African Americans to display or make obvious a countenance that would be perceived as disrespectful to a white person.[320] This could have contributed to Seymour's meekness.

---

[319] Many of the authors may have taken a biased approach in their interpretation.
[320] Jim Crow laws required that an African American person "never suggest that a White person is from an inferior class." Kennedy, *Jim Crow Guide*, 216–217.

The cultural differences between Seymour and Parham are evident; the exposure to social injustice by one and the privilege of the other made for a rather dysfunctional affiliation. Seymour and Parham's initial meeting was not on equal footing.[321] Therefore, if any friendship were to evolve, it would have had to be initiated by the authoritarian, which in this case was Parham. The doctrine of God was the core of their bond. Much of what was being taught by both men faced some interpretational challenges; however, many of the core principles are embraced by some mainline denominations today. The Azusa Street Mission overshadowed Parham's partial renditions of scripture, and Pentecostal leaders began to "reflect more self-consciously than they had before on the significance of race within the movement."[322] It would be fair to say that the Azusa Street Mission played a significant part in the discarding of the bigoted interpretations of the scriptures.

Bearing in mind all of the information gathered on these two men, there are three components to this relationship that must be considered. First, the racial component, which deals with individual barriers and laws enforcing segregation, must be examined; second, the cultural component and its effects on biblical interpretation and worship practice must be considered; and finally, the theological component, which is the handling of the doctrine of God, must be examined. Each of these components plays a substantial part in the relationship between Seymour and Parham.

6.1 THE RACIAL COMPONENT

Taking into account the strict segregation laws that were in place, we find that relationships between blacks and whites were not conventional. Since a relationship involves a connection of persons or the state of being connected, this would have acknowledged equality, which ran counter to the Jim Crow laws. The Jim Crow laws served as a deterrent to blacks who pursued equality and to whites who sought to form authentic friendships with blacks. On the other hand, the Jim Crow laws often served as an

---
321 See chapter 3 entitled "Relationship and Conflict."
322 Jacobsen, *Thinking in the Spirit*, 260.

excuse for some whites to hide behind, permitting them to harbor their contempt for those whom they deemed the inferior race. To deny assistance or a kind gesture for the sake of legislation defies morality and most certainly resists the tenets of Christianity. Those who preceded Parham—Wesley, Wilberforce, Lincoln, and Dowie—all acknowledged that racism was wrong.[323] Borlase insists, "When it comes to the question of Parham's racism, the trouble is that guys like him were supposed to play by a different set of rules."[324]

The word *racism* can be defined as "a learned belief in racial superiority, which includes the belief that race determines intellectual, cultural, and moral capacities."[325] Although racism was considered the norm in the early nineteenth century, one would immediately assume Christians would have made a concerted effort to liberate those being discriminated against rather than keeping them in bondage. A closer look, however, finds that those harboring racist beliefs were themselves captive to a type of bondage, rendering them incapable of freeing others. In most cases, racist rhetoric was being enacted by "White Christians justifying the enslavement of Blacks by abusing or ignoring the testimony of Scripture."[326] According to Borlase, "Power was a key jewel for the white preacher."[327] Clement of Alexandria,[328] a learned Christian teacher, was resolute in his stance against racism: "We admit that the same nature exists in every race, and the same virtue."[329] Obviously borrowing from the scriptures, Clement expresses the heart of Christ when he states, "At the same time,

---

323 Borlase, *William Seymour*, 83.
324 Ibid.
325 C. D. McConnell, "Racism," in *Evangelical Dictionary of Theology: Second Edition*, ed. Walter A. Elwell (Grand Rapids: Baker Academic, 2001), 978.
326 Gary A. Parrett. "Racism," in *Evangelical Dictionary of Christian Education*, ed. Michael J. Anthony (Grand Rapids: Baker Academic, 2001), 577.
327 Borlase, *William Seymour*, 84.
328 W. C. Weinrich, "Clement of Alexandria" in *Evangelical Dictionary of Theology: Second Edition*, 272.
329 "Clement of Alexandria" in *A Dictionary of Early Christian Beliefs*, ed. David W. Bercot (Peabody, MA: Hendrickson Publishing, 1998), 551.

it teaches us not to wrong anyone belonging to another race and to bring him under the yoke. For there is no other reason to justify such a thing than difference of race. But that is no reason at all."[330] Those who are a part of the body of Christ concede there is no distinction between people. The apostle Paul communicated the equalization of all people in Christ: "Here there is not Greek and Jew, circumcised and uncircumcised, barbarian, Scythian, slave, free; but Christ is all, and in all" (Col. 3:11, emphasis mine). "This passage is significant because it shows that Christ has removed four kinds of distinctions: national distinction (Greek or Jew), religious distinction (circumcised or uncircumcised), cultural distinction (barbarian or Scythian), and economic distinction (slave or free)."[331]

It is evident in the era of Seymour and Parham that two primary forms of racism were at play—individual and institutional—which are both generally viewed as products of either psychological or social forces.[332] Many of the arguments levied against Parham about his racism center around his outburst at the Azusa Street Mission. Prior to his outburst, Parham allowed Seymour to sit and listen to class lectures, accompanied him to the black districts of Houston to preach the gospel, and equipped Seymour with the necessary credentials to fulfill his ministry in Los Angeles. One fact still remained: Seymour was a black man.

If one were to make the case that Parham sought to make Seymour feel befriended, the Azusa Street rant would dispel any notion that this intention was real. "Racism can take on various forms, it can be overt or subtle, and can be practiced knowingly or unknowingly."[333] One of the major problems with racism is identifying it. Not everyone who disagrees or dislikes someone of another race is a racist. Parham's meltdown at Azusa and his racial comments preceding it exposed his prejudice. His dealings with Seymour prior to Azusa also can be attributed to other factors—such as pride, contention, and selfish ambition.

---

330 "Clement of Alexandria," in *A Dictionary of Early Christian Beliefs*, 551.
331 Anderson, *Christian Ethics in Plain Language*, 177.
332 McConnell, "Racism," 978.
333 Parrett, "Racism," 577.

Though Seymour has been portrayed as one who was meek in spirit, a number of occurrences caused him to ultimately fold under the racial tension being hurled at him from all sides. After Parham's visit to Azusa, William H. Durham attempted to form a coup to take over the Azusa Street Mission. The embezzlement of the Azusa mailing list by Clara Lum crippled the ministry financially, which eventually resulted in the decline of membership. During the final days of the Azusa Street Mission, Seymour started to show signs of racism. The constant betrayal from Seymour's white colleagues pushed him to rid the mission of those whom he felt were a hindrance to the flock of God. According to Newman, "Seymour proposed a measure intended to prevent further racial discord. On May 19, 1914, The Azusa Street Mission unanimously adopted a resolution that allowed only 'people of color' were to fill leadership roles."[334]

Although Seymour remained adamant that black and white brethren must love one another, it appears that the hurt he sustained was substantial enough to segregate. "The lives and ministries of Charles Parham and William Seymour epitomized the racial conflict that contributed to the fragmentation of the Pentecostal movement."[335] Racism is birthed out of fear. Anything outside of our realm of comfort is foreign, and accepting racial or cultural differences can appear to be harmful, even dangerous. Blacks, as well as other minorities, partake in the oppressive system of prejudice. "Most white Americans rarely consider the impact of this dimension of the problem because they have never suffered through the experience. White Americans do not suffer discrimination because of ideas that nonwhite persons have of them."[336] No race is exempt from character flaws, "for all have sinned and fall short of the glory of God"

---

334 Newman, *Race and the Assemblies of God Church*, 60. See also William Seymour, *The Doctrines and Disciplines of the Azusa Street: Apostolic Faith Mission of Los Angeles, California* (Joplin, MO: Christian Books, 2000), 48.
335 Newman, *Race and the Assemblies of God Church*, 62.
336 William Pannell, "Racism," in *The Complete Book of Everyday Christianity*, ed. Robert Banks and R. Paul Stevens (Downers Grove, IL: InterVarsity Press, 1997), 838–839.

(Rom. 3:23, emphasis mine). "Racism is a sin and, as such, racist beliefs and practices betray the very nature of God and the unity of creation."[337] Despite the rhetoric of those infusing Christianity with racism, race has no spiritual significance in the Bible. "In Christ the ground has been completely leveled. Every oppressive system of prejudice that people have established is disarmed and condemned."[338] Seymour and Parham were pioneers in their own right, yet the role Seymour could have played in the future of the Pentecostal movement was diminished by racial prejudice.[339] Parham, on the other hand, "missed the battle against injustice that was ahead of him. Had he played things differently, who knows where the church would be today."[340] As it has for ages, the division between race and culture continues to this day.

6.2 THE CULTURAL COMPONENT

It is not uncommon for one to look to a particular people or social group as the source of a specific type of culture. In times past, music was primarily viewed as black music and white music, but today the music industry is inundated with diversity. Its culture has shifted from being based in race to being focused on certain categories of music. For example, hip-hop, or rap, has not only broken down racial barriers but has also produced its own culture, dress, talk, and ideology. The church too has adapted culture to its own nature. According to Parrett, "A local church may proclaim that their doors are open to all people, regardless of race or color. But, in subtle or not-so-subtle ways, the church may communicate to newcomers that genuine acceptance into the fellowship and real opportunity for service and leadership are dependent upon willingness to lay aside key aspects of their own culture and behave as though they were members of the majority group."[341]

---

337 McConnell, "Racism," 978.
338 Parrett, "Racism," 578.
339 Martin, *The Life and Ministry of William J. Seymour*, 325.
340 Borlase, *William Seymour: A Biography*, 84.
341 Parrett, "Racism," 577.

The worship at Azusa Street was monumental as well as controversial; the congregation was made up of various races—African Americans, Latinos, Swedes, Italians, Armenians, Native Americans, Japanese, Russians, Germans, and Chinese. "At a time when most of American institutions, including churches, were rigidly segregated, Seymour's movement was remarkable for its interracial composition."[342] In fact, it has been reported by some that white congregants outnumbered blacks at the Azusa Street Mission.

Although the culture at Azusa had become multiethnic, the worship practice was predominantly African American. Much of the mission's music, preaching, and prayer life was contributed by whites and blacks who had frequented revivalist camp meetings.[343] Robeck insists this: "It would be unfair to claim that the only influence that played a role at the mission was the African American one—non-African Americans did bring their own gifts and experiences."[344]

Parham did not believe the spiritual culture at Azusa—the shouting, shivering, falling down, and shaking—was an appropriate reaction to God's presence. This would lead one to believe that Parham's congregants did not express the baptism of the Holy Spirit in this way. In fact, Parham referred to the behavior at Azusa as a "darkie revival" and at times made references to it being demonic. Parham's use of racial stereotypes reflects a sense of unfamiliarity with the African American worship culture and suggests imprudence masked by racism.

The religious experience of African Americans has deep and painful roots. The freedom to shout, shiver, fall down, and shake was not always afforded to blacks. To simply pray resulted in being flogged. Slaves would go to great lengths to worship: "Kalvin Wood remembered preaching to other slaves and singing and praying while huddled behind quilts and rags, which had been thoroughly wetted 'to keep the sound of their voices from penetrating the air' and then hung up 'in the form of a little room,' or

---

342 Sanders, *William Joseph Seymour*, 1.
343 Robeck Jr., *The Azusa Street Mission and Revival*, 138.
344 Ibid., 138.

tabernacle."[345] This was just one of many techniques used to deaden the sound and conceal it from their masters. A pot placed upside down and slightly propped up in the middle of the floor or doorstep would serve as a method for catching the sound of praying and singing. The image of a preacher kneeling over a kettle of water speaking (in hopes of drowning out the sound) surrounded by a circle of kneeling worshippers was a common occurrence on a certain plantation in Louisiana.[346] Once they were able to steal away, the slaves would unleash an overwhelming abundance of praise and worship. It was then that sufferings were forgotten and that the Holy Spirit could be fully embraced. They were free from kettles, pots, wet quilts, and rags. The presence of the Holy Spirit was felt at such a magnitude that it was hard to doubt that such a move of God would not provide reasons to shout, sing, and fall down. However, that was then. Today many wonder if what once was an authentic culture of worship has become a routine style of worship. An ex-slave declared this: "Meetings back there meant more than they do now. Then, everybody's heart was in tune, and when they called out on God, they made heaven ring. It was more than just Sunday meeting and then no godliness for a week."[347]

People have scrutinized the events that occurred at Azusa as much as they have esteemed these events. Nonetheless, the questions of skeptics remain: Was the reaction of the congregation an authentic reaction to the move of the Holy Spirit? Or were they, as Parrett stated, laying aside key aspects of their own culture and behaving as though they were members of the majority group? The human aspect cannot be excluded from the Azusa Street Mission: excessive enthusiasm may have played a role in the worship experience. Brumback says the following:

> Is it not at this point that fanaticism has crept in? Although God may make such a mighty impact upon a believer that his normal reaction takes some form of bodily exercise—shouting, trembling,

---

345 Raboteau, *Slave Religion*, 215.
346 Ibid.
347 Raboteau, *Slave Religion*, 217.

leaping, dancing, falling prostrate (all of these reactions occurred in biblical experiences which were genuinely inspired of God)—the danger occurs when the believer conceives the idea that all subsequent responses to the blessing of the Lord must follow the exact pattern of the initial reaction, whereas the God of variety does not always desire the identical reaction. Fanaticism is continuing to move after the Spirit has stopped.[348]

Charles Parham, on the other hand, was a product of a much different culture—one that did not include oppression or a constant fear of death at the hands of a system that encouraged oppression. Parham's actions and doctrine—particularly his racial views, which many of his contemporaries found to be viable—have earned him much criticism. Keep in mind that Parham was born into a culture that supported strong racial segregation and that all media, literature, mainstream churches, and educational teachings were racially biased at that time. Most whites then did not as readily view the plight of African Americans as horrifying like many people do today. This could possibly support the idea of Parham's inexperience with the black worship experience—hence the term "darkie revival." Often "God chooses what is foolish in the world to shame the wise; choosing what is weak in the world to shame the strong" (1 Cor. 1:27, emphasis mine). Simply put, God lifts up the downtrodden and inhabits the praise of those who genuinely cry out to Him. Scripture is riddled with many instances of those who suffered oppression under the hands of the elite being freed by God.

"Culture in the broadest sense is everything that people do with creation. It refers to the little worlds we make (through our own creativity in work, play and daily relationship) out of God's creation."[349] It is not uncommon to hear adverse talk about certain cultures, and in some cases,

---

348 Carl Brumback, Suddenly, from Heaven: A History of The Assemblies of God (Springfield, MO: Gospel Publishing House, 1961), 111.
349 Loren Wilkinson, "Culture," in *The Complete Book of Everyday Christianity*, eds. Robert Banks and R. Paul Stevens (Downers Grove, IL: InterVarsity Press, 1997), 257.

certain cultures can be met with a positive discourse. "Nor should it be surprising that Christians in different times and situations have tended to stress one set of texts about culture at the expense of another, with the result that the Scriptural ambivalence about culture has manifested itself in a variety of Christian understanding."[350] The societal norms of Seymour and Parham's time had a large impact on the behavior and attitudes of all races. Robeck claims, "Perhaps Seymour had learned the type of humility and submission he exercised at the mission from societal norms to which he was subject as an African American. It would have been extremely difficult for a black man to lord it over a white man at that time. But then again, Jesus was a gentle leader, directing with soft words, and Seymour was a man who spent much time in prayer with his Lord."[351]

Aside from all of the accusations lobbed at Parham, he had an undeniable love for God. No matter how misdirected his actions may have appeared, his love for God was always apparent. His aversion for Azusa, however, was unending. According to Newman, "Charles Parham was unable to embrace the interracial character of the Azusa Street revival. Later, he became an ardent supporter of the Ku Klux Klan and sought its support for his efforts to restore 'Old Time Religion' in American society."[352] The Azusa Street impasse made it clear that the cultural divide between Seymour and Parham was unmistakable, and if there was any relationship or friendship between the two, it eventually expired.

Theology was a significant part of the narrative between Seymour and Parham. The theological concepts of the Apostolic Faith Movement were formulated and instituted by Parham. The interpretational challenges surrounding most of Parham's doctrinal beliefs had no scriptural basis, leaving them unsubstantiated. Parham believed that the annihilation of the

---

350 Wilkinson, "Culture," 259.
351 Robeck Jr., *The Azusa Street Mission and Revival*, 93.
352 Newman, Race and the Assemblies of God Church, 58. Jacobsen also states, "Later in his life he went so far as to praise the Ku Klux Klan." Jacobsen, Thinking in the Spirit, 261.

unredeemed was a form of eternal punishment. He also believed that "race mixing" was the primary cause of the flood and that Abel's wife was of an inferior race. His view about Noah's curse on Canaan mirrors that of Abraham Kuyper.[353] McConnell insists, "The erroneous use of theological justification for racism is a perennial problem, for example, the use of Abraham Kuyper's concept of creation as pluriform to justify apartheid or use of Noah's curse on Canaan as a means of justifying slavery."[354]

6.3 THE THEOLOGICAL COMPONENT

Exegesis[355] was definitely not Parham's strong suit; on the other hand, eisegesis seemed to have been his method of choice. This is seen in Parham's ability to pour into the text his own presuppositions and biases. The term *exegesis* is derived from the Greek, which means "to lead" or "to explain." The word *eisegesis* means simply "into." ("Reading into the text" is a common phrase used when referring to this method.) The "eisegete" has no regard for interpretational fundamentals and therefore leaves his or her theories devoid of facts. The "exegete"[356] is committed to making a concerted effort to explain the text after careful consideration of the text. This can be seen as objective. Many of Parham's beliefs—especially those concerning race—were subjective. Somehow, in the middle of it all, Parham nailed down three doctrines, which became the underpinning of the Pentecostal movement. According to Goff, "Charles Parham fused three theological planks into the first Pentecostal doctrine: 1) Tongue speaking as the initial evidence of the Holy Spirit baptism, 2) Spirit-filled believers as the 'sealed' Bride of Christ, and 3) Xenoglossic

---

353 I. Hexham, "Kuyper, Abraham," in *Evangelical Dictionary of Theology: Second Edition*, ed. Walter A. Elwell (Grand Rapids: Baker Academic, 2001), 667.

354 McConnell, "Racism," 978.

355 "The act of explaining a text, in theology usually a sacred text. The purpose may be either to describe the author's meaning or to apply that meaning to a contemporary situation." E. A. Livingstone, *Oxford Concise Dictionary of the Christian Church* (Oxford: Oxford University Press, 2006), 209.

356 The term "exegete" is the name given to the expounder or interpreter; the term "eisegete," however, is typically used as an insult.

tongues as the tool for a dramatic end-time revival. Parham retained all three beliefs throughout his lifetime, but Pentecostals after 1910 have gradually rejected the last two."[357]

Though Parham contributed some significant dogma to the movement, his controversial racist interpretations of scripture were not widely accepted by most Pentecostal denominations. Jacobsen recognizes this: "Individuals such as Parham were not typical, however, and his views should not be used to paint the whole Pentecostal movement as backwoods, bigoted, and racist."[358] Once Seymour was able to shed his own beliefs regarding sanctification, the theological component of Seymour and Parham's relationship was harmonious in the early stages.[359] Notwithstanding Parham's racial dogma, Seymour accepted Parham's third blessing wholeheartedly. Parham's visit to Azusa along with the behavioral activities of others caused Seymour to rethink not only his relationships to those whom he esteemed but also the theology he had passionately embraced. It had become apparent to Seymour that racism was still an issue for the whites who had received the third blessing, which was speaking in tongues, and this led him to question the belief that speaking in tongues was the sign or the evidence of the baptism of the Holy Spirit. Rather, he felt that the abolishment of hatred and bitterness would be a much richer indicator or evidence of the baptism of the Holy Spirit.

In this particular case, scripture stands on Seymour's side. The fruit of the Holy Spirit is evident in scripture: "The fruit of the Spirit is love, joy, peace, patience, kindness, goodness, faithfulness, gentleness and self-control" (Gal. 5:22–23, emphasis mine). Those who possess the Holy Spirit exhibit these attributes. In contrast, "now the works of the flesh are evident: sexual immorality, impurity, sensuality, idolatry, sorcery, enmity, strife, jealousy, fits of anger, rivalries, dissensions, divisions, envy, drunkenness, orgies, and things like these. I warn you, as I warned you before,

---

357 Goff Jr., *Fields White unto Harvest*, 173.
358 Jacobsen, *Thinking in the Spirit*, 261.
359 The Holy Spirit is received at the time of sanctification. See chapter 2.

that those who do such things will not inherit the kingdom of God" (Gal. 5:19–21, emphasis mine).

Boice insists this: "If one's conduct is characterized by the traits in this list, then he or she is either not a believer or else a believer who is not being led by God's Spirit."[360] Seymour's newfound theory of a more evidential sign was met with an insensitive retort.[361] Experience rather than theology appeared to be at the forefront of this particular movement at the time. As long as one was able to speak in tongues, it was evident that the baptism of the Holy Spirit was complete. This negates many Bible verses, such as 1 Corinthians 13:1, which says, "If I speak in the tongues of men and of angels, but have not love, I am a noisy gong or a clanging cymbal" (emphasis mine). The absence of love leads to egocentrism, which leads to one wounding those in his or her path. "Christian love is a gift from God, demonstrated supremely in the cross (see Rom. 5:8). God's love always takes the initiative, and the love of Christians is a response to that love."[362] Jacobsen warns of the danger of experience without theology: "Within early Pentecostalism, theology and experience went hand in hand. There is no doubt that experience was a crucial dimension of the early Pentecostal movement, but it was experience guided by theological truth that really mattered. Experience alone was considered dangerous."[363] In the case of Seymour, the lack of the theological component in the doctrine of speaking in tongues pushed him away from relationships and a belief system that he had once cherished.

These three components—racial, cultural, and theological—provide a framework for a concise analysis of Seymour and Parham's relationship. Although numerous reports attribute much of the dissent to Parham, Seymour later gave in to the antagonism by eventually moving the mission

---

360 James Montgomery Boice, "Galatians," in *The Expositor's Bible Commentary*, ed. Frank E. Gaebelein (Grand Rapids: Baker Academic, 1976), 496.
361 See chapter 1 entitled "The Story."
362 Robert W. Yarbrough, ESV Study Bible (Wheaton, IL: Crossways Bibles, 2008), 2436.
363 Jacobsen, *Thinking in the Spirit*, 3.

in the direction of segregation. "The historical memory of Seymour's leadership disappeared, but the fact remains that the Pentecostal/Charismatic renewal movement began among the black people under the leadership of a black man."[364] The relational conflict between Seymour and Parham stands as a testament to many that God is faithful despite human differences. Pentecostalism today is "the fastest growing Christianity in the world, and the raw numbers are huge. Current estimates are more than five hundred million adherents worldwide."[365] The ignorance and indecisiveness of humans cannot prevent or hinder the accomplishing of God's will.

---

364 Sanders, *William Joseph Seymour*, 130.
365 Jacobsen, *Thinking in the Spirit*, ix.

Bibliography

The Apostolic Faith (Portland, Oregon), July and August 1908.

Alexander, Michelle. *The New Jim Crow: Mass Incarceration in the Age of Colorblindness.* New York: The New Press, 2010.

Anderson, Kerby. *Christian Ethics in Plain Language.* Nashville: Thomas Nelson, 2005.

Arnold, Clinton E. *Acts.* Grand Rapids: Zondervan, 2002.

Bartleman, Frank. *Azusa Street.* New Kingston, PA: Whitaker House, 1982.

Boice, James Montgomery. "Galatians." In *The Expositor's Bible Commentary*, edited by Frank E. Gaebelein. Grand Rapids: Baker Academic, 1976.

Borlase, Craig. *William Seymour: A Biography.* Lake Mary, FL: Charisma House, 2006.

Brand, W. C. "The Effects of the Tongues Movement." in *The Religious World Looks at Azusa Street 1906–1907: Skeptics & Scoffers*, edited by Larry E. Martin. Pensacola, FL: Christian Life Books, 2004.

Broussard, Bernard. *A History of St. Mary Parish.* Unpublished manuscript, 1955.

Brumback, Carl. *Suddenly, From Heaven: A History of The Assemblies of God.* Springfield, MO: Gospel Publishing House, 1961.

Butler, Trent C. "Gift of Tongues," in *Holman Bible Dictionary*, edited by Trent C. Butler, Nashville: Holman Bible Publishers, 1991.

"Clement of Alexandria." In *A Dictionary of Early Christian Beliefs*, edited by David W. Bercot. Peabody, MA: Hendrickson Publishing, 1998.

Clemmons, Ithiel C. *Bishop C. H. Mason and the Roots of the Church of God and Christ.* Bakersfield, CA: Pneuma Life Publishing, 1996. Kindle edition.

Craigie, William A., and James R. Hulbert, eds., *A Dictionary of American English on Historical Principles*, Chicago: University of Chicago Press, 1938–1944.

"Creation and Formation. *Houston Daily Post*, August 13, 1905.

Cox, Harvey. *Fire from Heaven: The Rise of Pentecostal Spirituality and the Reshaping of Religion in the Twenty-First Century.* Reading, MA: Addison-Wesley Publishing, 1995.

Duffield, Guy P., and N. M. Van Cleave. *Foundations of Pentecostal Theology*, San Dimas, California: L.I.F.E. Bible College at Los Angeles, 1987.

Faupel, William D. *The Everlasting Gospel: The Significance of Eschatology in the Development of Pentecostal Thought.* Sheffield, England: Sheffield Academic Press, 1996.

Garraty, John A. *The American Nation to 1877: A History of the United States.* New York: Harper and Row, 1963.

Goff, J. R., Jr. "Charles Fox Parham." In *Dictionary of Pentecostal and Charismatic Movements*, edited by Stanley M. Burgess, Gary B. McGee, and Patrick H. Alexander. Grand Rapids: Zondervan Publishing House, 1988.

Goff, James R., Jr. *Fields White unto Harvest: Charles F. Parham and the Missionary Origins of Pentecostalism*. Fayetteville, AR: University of Arkansas Press, 1988.

Helm, Bennett. "Friendship," in *The Stanford Encyclopedia of Philosophy*, edited by Edward N. Zalta. http://plato.stanford.edu/archives/fall2009/entries/friendship.

Hexham, I. "Kuyper, Abraham." In *Evangelical Dictionary of Theology: Second Edition*, edited by Walter A. Elwell. Grand Rapids: Baker Academic, 2001.

Hollenweger, Walter J. *Pentecostalism: Origins and Developments Worldwide*. Peabody, MA: Hendrickson Publishers, 1997.

Hunt, John, ed., *The Essential Writings of the American Black Church*. Chattanooga, TN: AMG Publishers, 2008.

Jacobsen, Douglas. *Thinking in the Spirit: Theologies of the Early Pentecostal Movement*. Bloomington, Indiana: Indiana University Press, 2003.

Jenkins, Joanna. *General Affidavit*, June 14, 1893, Simon Seymour Pension File. National Archives and Records Administration.

Joyner, Rick. *Azusa Street: The Fire That Could Not Die*. http://www.openheaven.com/library/history/azusa.htm.

Kelsey, Morton. *Tongue Speaking: An Experiment in Spiritual Experience*. Garden City, NY: Doubleday, 1964.

Kennedy, Stetson. *Jim Crow Guide: The Way It Was*. Boca Raton, FL: Florida Atlantic University Press, 1959.

Livingstone, E. A. *Oxford Concise Dictionary of the Christian Church.* Oxford: Oxford University Press, 2006.

Lum, Clara. "Clara Lum Writes Wonders." *The Missionary World* (1906).

Martin, Larry E. *The Life and Ministry of William J. Seymour: And a History of the Azusa Street Revival.* Pensacola, FL: Christian Life Books, 2006.

McConnell, C. D. "Racism." In *Evangelical Dictionary of Theology: Second Edition*, edited by Walter A. Elwell. Grand Rapids: Baker Academic, 2001.

Melton, Gordon J. *Encyclopedia of American Religion: Fourth Edition Supplement.* Detroit: Gale Research Inc., 1994.

Nelson, J. D. "For Such a Time as This: The Study of Bishop William Seymour and the Azusa Street Revival." PhD diss., University of Birmingham, England, 1981.

Newman, Joe. *Race and the Assemblies of God Church: The Journey from Azusa Street to the "Miracle of Memphis."* Youngstown, New York: Cambria Press, 2007.

Olsen, Ted. "American Pentecost: The Story behind the Azusa Street Revival, the Most Phenomenal Event of Twentieth-Century Christianity." *Christian History* XVII, no. 58 (1998): 45.

Packard, Jerrold M. *American Nightmare: The History of Jim Crow.* New York: St. Martin's Press, 2002.

Pannell, William. "Racism." In *The Complete Book of Everyday Christianity*, edited by Robert Banks and R. Paul Stevens. Downers Grove, IL: InterVarsity Press, 1997.

Parham, Charles F. "God's Plan of the Ages." *Gospel of the Kingdom* (1910).

Parham, Charles F. *Kol Kare Bomidbar: A Voice Crying in the Wilderness.* Baxter Springs, KS: Apostolic Faith Bible College.

Parham, Charles F. *The Everlasting Gospel.* Baxter Springs, KS: Apostolic Faith Bible College.

Parham, Sarah E. *The Life of Charles F. Parham: Founder of the Apostolic Faith Movement.* New York: Garland Publication, 1985.

Parrett, Gary A. "Racism." In *Evangelical Dictionary of Christian Education*, ed. Michael J. Anthony. Grand Rapids: Baker Academic, 2001.

Pennington, W. C. James. "Great Moral Dilemma," in *African American Religious History: a Documentary Witness, Second Edition*, edited by Milton C. Sernett. London: Duke University Press, 1999.

Pilgrim, David. "What was Jim Crow?" Jim Crow Museum of Racist Memorabilia. Oct. 10, 2011. www.ferris.edu/jimcrow/what.htm.

Raboteau, Albert J. *Slave Religion: The Invisible Institution in the Antebellum South.* Oxford: Oxford University Press, 1978.

Randolph, Peter. "Plantation Churches: Visible and Invisible." In *African American Religious History: A Documentary Witness, Second Edition*, edited by Milton C. Sernett. London: Duke University Press, 1999.

Robeck, C. M., Jr. *The Azusa Street Mission and Revival: The Birth of the Global Pentecostal Movement.* Nashville: Thomas Nelson Inc., 2006.

Robeck, C. M., Jr. "Warren Fay Carothers." In *Dictionary of Pentecostal and Charismatic Movements*, edited by Stanley M. Burgess, Gary B. McGee, and Patrick H. Alexander. Grand Rapids: Zondervan Publishing House, 1988.

Rutty, Jennie C. "The Gift of Tongues." *The Gospel Trumpet*, September 18, 1902.

Sanders, Rufus G. W. *William Joseph Seymour: Father of the 20th Century Pentecostal/Charismatic Movement.* Sandusky, OH: Alexandria Publications, 2003.

Synan, H. V. "William J. Seymour," in *Dictionary of Pentecostal and Charismatic Movements.* Edited by Stanley M. Burgess, Gary B. McGee, and Patrick H. Alexander. Grand Rapids: Zondervan Publishing House, 1988.

Synan, Vinson, and Charles R. Fox Jr., *William J. Seymour: Pioneer of the Azusa Street Revival.* Alachua, FL: Bridge-Logos Foundation, 2012.

Seymour, William. *The Doctrines and Disciplines of the Azusa Street: Apostolic Faith Mission of Los Angeles, California.* Joplin, MO: Christian Books, 2000.

Thrapp, Dan L. "Pentecostal Sects to Convene Here." *Los Angeles Times* (Los Angeles, CA), Sept. 9, 1956.

Tinney, James S., and Stephen N. Short, eds. *In the Tradition of William J. Seymour: Essays Commemorating the Dedication of Seymour House at Howard University.* Washington, DC: Spirit Press, 1978.

Valdez, A. C., Sr., and James F. Scheer, *Fire on Azusa Street.* Costa Mesa, CA: Gift Publications, 1980.

White, Alma. *My Heart and My Husband.* Zarephath, NJ: Pillar of Fire Publishers, 1923.

Wilkinson, Loren. "Culture." In *The Complete Book of Everyday Christianity*, edited by Robert Banks and R. Paul Stevens. Downers Grove, IL: InterVarsity Press, 1997.

"Women with Men Embrace," *The Los Angeles Daily* Times, Sept. 3, 1906, 11.

Yarbrough, Robert W. *ESV Study Bible.* Wheaton, IL: Crossways Bibles, 2008.

About the Author

James D. Croone Sr. serves as an adjunct professor at Northwest University and an Education Specialist at the Seattle Union Gospel Mission. His other pursuits include leading an enhanced Bible Study in South Seattle (Friday Night Light), teaching New and Old Testament studies, and Urban Missions. Dr. Croone holds a D.R.E degree from A.L. Hardy Academy of Theology and a MATC from Northwest University.

Made in the USA
San Bernardino, CA
21 March 2017